THE FINAL COUNTDOWN
*Strategies To Reach The Third Stage Of
Digital Transformation*

ERIC KIMBERLING

Copyright © 2023
ERIC KIMBERLING
The Final Countdown
*Strategies To Reach The Third Stage Of
Digital Transformation*
All rights reserved.

No part of this publication may be reproduced, distributed, or transmitted in any form or by any means, including photocopying, recording, or other electronic or mechanical methods, without the prior written permission of the publisher, except in the case of brief quotations embodied in critical reviews and certain other non-commercial uses permitted by copyright law.

ERIC KIMBERLING

First Edition 2023

Table of Contents

Foreword 1
Chapter 1 4
    Don't Be a Case Study
Chapter 2 8
    Digital Strategy in the Era of All Things Digital
Chapter 3 13
    Constructing a Winning Digital Transformation Strategy
PART I 23
    Processes
Chapter 4 24
    Bridging the Gap
Chapter 5 33
    Process Improvements
Chapter 6 40
    Defining Performance Metrics
Chapter 7 44
    How do Processes Change People and Technology
Chapter 8 47
    Next Steps: Perform an Operational Assessment
PART II 53
    People
Chapter 9 54
    Why Organizational Change Management Matters
Chapter 10 62
    Understanding Resistance to Change
Chapter 11 72
    The Power of Company Culture
Chapter 12 85
    Organizational Alignment
Chapter 13 90
    Organizational Structure
Chapter 14 96
    Change Impact on People
Chapter 15 99
    How to Convey the Vision
Chapter 16 109
    Next Steps: Developing an Organizational Change Plan
PART III 112
    Technology

Chapter 17 113
    The Launching Pad
Chapter 18 120
    Visualizing The Future
Chapter 19 127
    The Guard Rails
Chapter 20 139
    Top Existing and Emerging Technologies in the Digital Era
Chapter 21 148
    Which Software is Right for You?
Chapter 22 163
    Implementation Planning
Chapter 23 180
    Countdown to Launch
Chapter 24 187
    Next Steps: Get Started on Software Implementation
Chapter 25 192
    Orbiting in the Third Stage
Acknowledgments 196
Citations 197

This book is dedicated to each one of you who has stood unwaveringly in the pursuit of transparency and the relentless endeavor to create change. Your unwavering belief in the power of truth, honesty, and accountability has been the driving force behind our collective journey towards more effective digital transformations.

Foreword

It was 2003 when Nike lost hundreds of millions of dollars. They had recently integrated a demand planning software that fell flat, reflecting the precise opposite of their market's demand. Their warehouse was stocked full of Air Garnett sneakers collecting dust and eating up warehouse space around the country. Meanwhile, the product that everyone wanted, Air Jordan sneakers, was missing from inventory, with production lead times spanning several months. Nike found itself in a predicament that kept them from accommodating its customers and, in turn, losing millions of dollars in sales. Nike stores across the world scrambled to meet their customer's needs as people poured in to buy the shoes glossed with Michael Jordan's name.

Air Jordan sneakers were in high demand, but the 'glitch' in Nike's demand planning software anticipated the demand of thousands more Air Garnett sneakers than Air Jordans. This miscalculation left a gap in supply, costing Nike millions of dollars in wasted inventory, lost sales, and operational inefficiency. The mishap didn't stop there. That so-called 'glitch' in their new demand planning software may have been closely tied to their factory productions overseas, but it had a residual impact that caused a domino effect spanning all aspects of the business. Such a large, miscalculated projection left its imprint on the balance sheet. The mark was visible enough that the loss had to be reported on their quarterly earnings call in order to stay compliant with the U.S.

Securities and Exchange Commission and maintain trust with shareholders. It was after that conference call that Nike's stock price dropped by a whopping 20%.

As a leader at the company around that time, it may have been hard to understand how a once shiny, new enterprise resource planning software, otherwise known as ERP software, could lead to such a catastrophic result. A 400 million dollar investment, a 20% dip in stock price, and a 100 million dollar loss between missed sales and over expenditures on inventory was something no executive at Nike would have ever imagined. So, what went wrong?

Nike had done their due diligence in implementation planning, but there were deep holes in its overarching digital strategy. Whether you're a titan corporation like Nike or a small business working to automate your processes by implementing new software, you are gambling if you embark on a digital transformation without an air-tight, comprehensive digital strategy. This book is intended to help business owners, executives, and project leaders get a holistic and full-scope grasp on the foundational elements that hold up a successful digital transformation. This book is for business and project leaders who do not want to make the same mistake that Nike made.

Many can count only on one hand how many software implementation projects they have been a part of, if any. The reality is that implementing software at one company looks completely different than it does at another, even if you are implementing the same software. The nature of the company, the company culture, the team's skill level, the processes, and the data management practices are all different from one company to the next.

Unless you are implementing new software on a regular basis, it's challenging to execute at a high level on every component of a digital transformation.

As you read through this book, you will grasp the framework needed to formulate and optimize your digital strategy. In the famous words of David Bowie, this is ground control, and you are Major Tom. These best practices have been tested across hundreds of industries with countless different software solutions. Each one has proven to help launch organizations to orbit - where all processes are streamlined and operational synergies are born. Only when a company reaches orbit will it be able to truly foster and develop its competitive advantage. These keys will guide your rocket to the stratosphere and enable your organization to grow in new and exciting ways.

It's important to note that the solutions in this book are not one-size-fits-all. These are not cookie-cutter solutions that apply evenly to every company. I encourage you to take each concept discussed in this book and apply it with the unique attributes of your company in mind. At the end of each section, there will be clearly defined steps that you can take to implement the contents and ideas of this book into your very own digital strategy. So long as you read this text through the lens of your own needs, it will guide you on your journey to the stratosphere.

The information in this book will provide you with an unbiased and unfiltered approach to building an untouchable digital strategy. It will help you define what a digital transformation will mean for your team, your processes, and your software solutions given your distinct company culture, operations, and system infrastructure. Your approach and determination of the elements in this book will be distinctive to your organization, so lean in to your own unique perspective as it relates to these topics.

With over twenty-five years of experience in helping organizations large and small find, implement, and optimize new enterprise software, I have garnered the ideologies, tactics, and best practices that my consulting group runs on. I am going to give you the secrets to formulating the blueprint that will lead to your company's ongoing success in utilizing and leveraging new-age technology. You will walk away with an unfiltered and unbiased perspective of what a digital strategy entails and be able to make decisions more confidently to keep your business competitive as technology continuously evolves. You'll also understand and be wary of the common causes that lead to ERP failure so you don't make expensive mistakes like Nike once did.

Here, you will harvest the best practices and key concepts that drive successful digital strategy and will walk away with a tangible action plan that can be implemented directly into your own business. Are you ready to strategically and intentionally launch your company into the dawn of a new digital era?

Let's dive in.

Chapter 1

Don't Be a Case Study

On average, a company spends between three and four percent of annual revenue on a digital transformation project to optimize operations and automate processes. Nike's digital transformation in 2003 had the same intent and roughly the same budget. At the time, Nike was north of a 10 billion dollar company[1], so spending 400 million on new software and everything that goes with it was fairly intuitive. What was not intuitive was their approach to the implementation.

If we were to ask Nike's leadership, this was nothing but a 'glitch' in their system. It was simply viewed as a speed bump in the grand scheme of their billion-dollar operation. The question here is, *was it really a speed bump, or could it have been avoided in its entirety?*

The issues Nike ran into were based on its inability to accurately forecast demand. They couldn't get the right product mix to their customers and were unable to fully grasp the demand to produce the right amount of product in each category. When they realized the fumble, long production lead times kept them from adjusting in time to mitigate the problem. Yes, it was the system that projected inaccurately. The system they implemented may have been too slow, maybe it didn't integrate well, or potentially had some bugs that needed to be worked through. However, at its core, there were three holes in Nike's approach during this digital transformation:

1. Nike's planners were inadequately trained on how to use the system before it went live.
2. Nike did not have a process in place for someone to check and confirm demand projections before the factory began production.

---

[1] "*Top 10 Digital Transformation Failures of All Time, Selected by an ERP Expert Witness*", Third Stage Consulting Group, April 8, 2021, Top 10 Digital Transformation Failures of All Time, Selected by an ERP Expert Witness - Third Stage Consulting (thirdstage-consulting.com)

3. Nike missed the target in their testing efforts. A bug of this size should have been caught during tests prior to going live.

Although there were some issues with the system, pinpointing the root cause of an ERP failure is done by peeling back layers of the subject's digital strategy. The success or failure of a digital strategy can be rooted in three pillars of a digital transformation: *People, processes,* and *technology.* Nike made mistakes on one component within each of these three pillars, and it was reflected as a $100 million loss. Opportunities were missed through a lack of comprehensive training (*People*), failure to implement revised workflows for newly launched software to keep demand planning systems in check (*Processes*), and neglect to run comprehensive, end-to-end testing to ensure glitches were caught and addressed before going live with the new software (*Technology*).

Three characteristics define failure when it comes to implementing enterprise software:

1. It costs more time or more money than originally expected.
2. It delivers considerably less business value than anticipated.
3. It sees operational or material disruption that affects your business.

Any of these three factors can be chalked up as an ERP failure. Unfortunately, Nike fell prey to all three, and they are still working to optimize their operations as a result. It's not just Nike. Believe it or not, over half of all organizations fail based on these standards. It's more common than one would think, and most of the time, it's due to a subpar or complete lack of a digital strategy to guide the transformation through common pitfalls every company faces when implementing enterprise software.

If there is no digital strategy, there is no north star. There are various common pitfalls that nearly all organizations run into through transformation projects. It's these pitfalls that can make or break a company's success. Of course, we have instances such as Nike's 2003 crash and burn, but other pitfalls dance their way into a project and leave project leaders scrambling to make up for lost time, lost capital, and operational disruptions.

The most common culprit is a lack of alignment across all executives in which direction the rocket is going. Oftentimes, this lack of alignment can be rooted in either miscommunication or more generically, in internal biases. For example, a company's objective may be to grow its bottom line. We can get to that result in a few different ways. If the CFO of the organization has their eye on cutting costs while the COO has the intention of driving revenue, there is a lack of alignment. Yes, each of these strategies serves as a pathway to drive the bottom line, but they are all unique pathways, nonetheless. The way we drive revenue within a company looks different than the way we cut costs. This misalignment in the *how* is the very thing that many companies face. So, before implementing any changes, we must ensure our team is aligned and facing the north star as one, cohesive unit as we formulate our digital strategy. That way, when it comes time for transformation, our team can ensure all sails are set in the same direction.

The lack of project governance is another huge pitfall that organizations run into. There are various, complex, and expensive decisions one must make when considering enterprise technology. While we are in the thick of a transformation project, we need guardrails to guide the challenges along the way. Formulating a comprehensive digital strategy can act as just that – the guard rails. When it comes time to determine which software to select or which modules we'll need to integrate, we can refer back to our digital strategy and recall what we initially set out to do. If it supports our digital strategy and inches the company closer to its overarching strategic objectives, then do it. If it doesn't, then don't.

Without a digital strategy, we neither garner executive alignment, nor will we have a means of governance. Without a digital strategy, we will get to the other side of the project and realize that we are no better off than we were before. Whether we classify as a Fortune 500 entity or a small business, the level at which we are prepared to launch a digital transformation is the level at which we will succeed. More time should be spent in planning and strategizing our roadmap than anywhere else in a given implementation project. The lack of an all-encompassing digital strategy guiding a software implementation puts us at risk and may only drive a wider gap between where we are today and where we want to go.

Each segment of this book will discuss various considerations that can be used to integrate our overarching corporate strategy into our digital strategy. That digital strategy will be our roadmap to the execution of our digital transformation. It will help drive the understanding of how we can optimize current operations utilizing modern technology. In today's digitized world, our corporate strategy and our digital strategy are nearly one and the same, and we cannot define one without the other. Without a synergistic vision and execution plan, it will be difficult to garner buy-in from our team, make sound business decisions, or stay relevant in the ever-changing digital world we live in today.

Chapter 2

Digital Strategy in the Era of All Things Digital

Today's world is driven by technology. Business operations are now defined by the level of technology that supplements the operating model. It's our enterprise software that helps track metrics, identify opportunities, maintain organization, and ultimately inch us ahead of our competition. Without a sound digital strategy in place, competitors will overbear the market and our business will dwindle. Without a clear vision of what we want our company to be when it grows up and how we want the organization to operate, it will be difficult to pinpoint technologies that can be leveraged to help us get there. A clear digital strategy should be the horse before the chariot that powers our digital transformation. It will enable us to maintain a competitive advantage as the world becomes more and more technologically advanced. It has never been more important to align our corporate and digital strategies to reach our target operating model.

Now, what exactly is a digital strategy? Let's simplify the concept and take the word 'digital' out of the picture. As an executive team, we likely have a strategy in place. Maybe our overarching strategy is to lead our industry in customer experience, or it could be that our company wants to build a reputation of having the quickest turnaround time in deliveries. This overarching business strategy is what will help our organization stand out against the others, and it will encompass the business aspects that our company is best positioned to execute. A digital strategy is a plan that an executive team must align on to determine *how* the company will achieve its established business strategy. *How* will we create a premier customer experience? *How* will we be able to deliver packages the fastest out of all our competitors? *How* will we increase the bottom line?

In the dark ages, or just fifty years ago, the *how* was entirely dependent on the people and the processes in place. Fast forward to the twenty-first century and technology has developed as the third piece to the puzzle that helps get organizations to their strategic goals. Our technology, processes, and people within our organization are married, with one unable to fully function without the other. It's the tripod to success, and the detailed compilation of each of those elements is what formulates a digital strategy.

Let's run through an example. Say an executive team has aligned on a strategic plan designed to drive revenue by cross-selling more products. They must take that specific strategic goal and work backward to formulate a digital strategy. To formulate the digital strategy, they must have a stronghold on how adding cross-selling metrics will affect their sales team, how the selling and closing processes will be altered to get there, and ultimately, which CRM, or customer relationship management tool, will help them optimize their cross-selling and upselling efforts. Their digital strategy will be the detailed roadmap that outlines *how* they will manage the people, processes, and technology in order to reach their company's strategic goals.

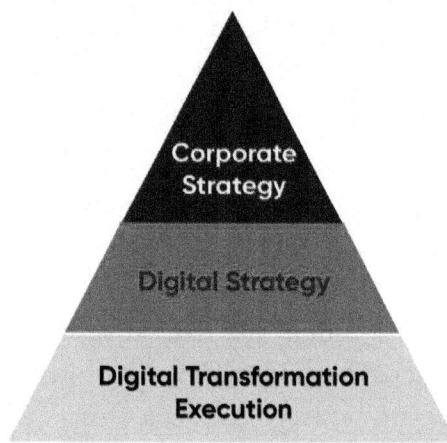

Translating our corporate strategy to an aligned digital strategy is called *strategy articulation*, and it requires us to dig below the surface to understand the complexities of the organizational, operational, and technological sides of our business. It also guides in planning tactics and practices that will optimize those elements. We do this through the development of a digital strategy. One of the most important things to understand is that an effective digital strategy is tailored for and aligned with an organization's specific needs.

Every organization has a unique culture, distinct operations, different competencies, and varying technological needs. Each organization's digital strategy needs to reflect the differentiators within its business. So, how do we do that for our business? The key is to envision how technology will enable us to reach our greater goals and objectives as an organization. If we have a clear strategic plan on a corporate level, it becomes easier to identify and outline the digital strategy that will pave the path for us to get there. We can prime ourselves to start constructing a cohesive digital strategy by pondering these six considerations:

Define who we are and where we are going.

Alignment with corporate strategy and culture is the most important aspect of an effective digital strategy. Understanding who we are as an entity today and who we want to be when our company matures is the single most important step before formulating any digital strategy and ultimately, implementing new software. If our digital strategy is aligned with our corporate strategy, then we have a high chance of success when we begin our digital transformation execution.

With this in mind, our first step is to define our core competencies and overarching corporate strategy for the future. What is it we are trying to accomplish as an organization? What is our vision for how our operations will look in the future? Do we have the best customer experience out of all our competitors? Do we make deliveries to consumers in record time? The answers to these and other questions will set us on the path toward formulating the best digital strategy possible.

Identify and improve processes and workstreams.

Once we understand where we are and where we are going as an organization, we will be able to pinpoint and prioritize the processes that need love. The processes that have bottlenecks or are too manual for efficiency's sake, the ones that stand as the biggest barrier to where we are today and where we want to be in the future – It's these processes that need to adapt and change. In chapter 5, we'll walk through the Hierarchy of Processes to help identify which processes to improve and how to improve upon them.

Establish project governance.

It is important to define what success means to us. This entails defining our key operational metrics, and those metrics should always be tied to the greater processes and results that move the needle toward our corporate strategy. These metrics will also help establish and maintain project governance and risk mitigation strategies. Above all else, they will help us justify and optimize the benefits of our potential digital strategies.

Build an organizational change management strategy to support our digital strategy.

Our digital strategy won't mean much without an effective organizational change management strategy to support it. After all, technology is just technology without a team of people running the show and inputting effective data. Strategizing the human component of a transformation is one of the most important inputs and determinants of success.

We'll get into how to clearly define an organizational change plan in Part II: People. To summarize, however, an organizational change plan should address organizational readiness, change impact, organizational design, and other critical activities that most project teams and system integrators don't think about.

Objectively consider the pros and cons of our potential software options.

An organization has several potential strategic alternatives, each with its distinct tradeoffs. No one alternative will be perfect, so we should never adopt the mentality that upgraded technology or improved processes will fix *everything*. There is no silver bullet that will solve all a problem in one pull, so it is important to objectively evaluate each avenue. The metrics and business case we define will help to evaluate the strengths and weaknesses of each route we could take.

For example, once we begin inching toward the software selection phase of a digital transformation, we may be weighing our options between SAP S/4HANA vs. Oracle Cloud ERP vs. Microsoft Dynamics 365 as potential solutions. Each will have different implementation costs, different impacts on our organization, and different tradeoffs. Each one will speak to the needs we have differently. The only way to make the right selection is to first prioritize our needs, our wants, and our expectations to evaluate each option objectively. We will discuss this further in chapter 22.

Outline an implementation plan that is aligned with our digital strategy.

After we do our due diligence in planning, researching, surveying, and optimizing what is our current state, we can pull everything together to create an implementation plan that will guide our digital transformation execution. Our implementation plan will define how each technical element of our digital strategy will unfold. We will marry our organizational change plan, our business process improvement plans, and our system implementation plan together as one. These facets of digital transformation make up the formula for a cohesive digital strategy, and only then are we ready to move forward with a software implementation.

As we cover the three pillars of digital strategy in the pages ahead, we will walk through each of the above considerations in more detail. By the time we've gone through all these concepts together, you'll walk away with a step-by-step action plan that will enable your organization to reach new heights, so long as it's used in synergy with your corporate strategy.

The best digital strategy for our organization looks unlike the best ones for most other companies. There are no generic answers, so it's important to objectively define what works for us. Only when we take an aerial view of each path will we understand which road is worth pursuing. Rather than spending money on implementing software, invest in a cohesive digital transformation strategy that will evolve and grow the organization. After all, that's what everyone is after. Isn't it?

Chapter 3

Constructing a Winning Digital Transformation Strategy

Digital transformation is a lot less like rolling out technology and a lot more like building a house. The execution of every component of a digital transformation – the process, the strategy, the implementation – entails some level of key work streams that will set a project up for success or failure. Similarly, the execution of every component of building a home – the process, the materials, the construction – entails some level of key work streams that will set the project up for success or failure. There are countless lessons we can learn from building a house and we can apply those lessons to our digital transformation journey.

One of the biggest pitfalls organizations trip on is the motivation to jump straight into deploying technology. They have identified their needs, defined what it is they want out of technology and dialed in on the technology solution or solutions that are the best fit for their organization. Since they have done those few things, they believe they are ready to jump straight into designing, building, and deploying the new software. This mindset is exactly what leads organizations into operational disruption, or worse, litigation against a software vendor.

To avoid those worst-case scenarios, we need a digital transformation blueprint. Rather than just defining our high-level business requirements, picking software, and then jumping straight into building stuff, we need to take the time upfront to cover phase zero of digital transformation – implementation readiness. We need to become crystal clear about what our future state business processes are going to be and what we want the future state organization to look like. Once we know where we want to be, we have to prepare our people and processes for that change. Without covering the first two pillars, the third pillar (technology) will fall flat.

Many times, software vendors and system integrators will suggest that we don't worry about the blueprint. "We'll help you," they say. Sure, they may help map out a blueprint to some degree, but it will primarily be focused on the technology pillar of the organization. They will help define how the software should be built, but they often lack the intricate details of managing people and optimizing processes to help our organization reach our targeted future state. A software vendor or integrator will be focused on software rather than the bigger picture of how a business is going to operate post-go-live.

Before we dive into the three pillars of digital strategy, it's important to be fully cognizant of the fact that technology is just one piece of the puzzle. All three pillars of digital transformation need to be incorporated into the greater digital strategy in order to reach our target operating model, or what we'll refer to as *orbit*. A sound and cohesive digital strategy will incorporate a blueprint for processes, people, *and* technology. Furthermore, it will be guided by the processes and people aspect of our organization rather than the technical aspect.

The likelihood of a siloed, technology-focused blueprint being aligned with an organization's business needs is very low. In fact, there is a higher chance of misalignment and falling into the never-ending cycle of playing catch up to reach the goals and objectives set forth at the beginning of the project when we try to fit our people and processes into technology rather than finding a technology that fits our people and processes. This is why we, as business and project leaders, need to take ownership of crafting and designing our blueprint.

Think about it. An architect or home builder would never come to the table with a blueprint that defines the future home as a two-story, 2,000-square-foot, single-family home. A new build construction would never start with plumbing. An electrician would never show up, unbriefed, to begin installing electrical outlets and running Cat5 cables as the first step to building a home from the ground up. There is not a single trade that would begin its work without first addressing the blueprint. Moreover, there is an order of operations that must be followed to ensure the structural integrity of the new build. The blueprint will act as a guide, a map. It will show how the house is to be built, in what order, and how all the different pieces and trades will fit together to reach a final product.

When we hire a software vendor or system integrator to come in and start deploying technology straight out the gate, we're essentially hiring a plumber as the first step to building a house. It's just something we don't do. If we were to do that, chances are pretty high that the home will have an unstable foundation and will not be built to code.

One of the most important things we can do as project leaders and executive sponsors is to take note of the timeless best practices that have worked for others. We must do it right. There is too much money, time, and energy poured into a digital transformation to skip certain elements of the greater project. Regardless of if we believe we can save time and money, or we simply are not aware of the right thing to do, we cannot risk doing this wrong.

The blueprint for what our business is going to look like in the future needs to be set in place *before* we select and implement software. The processes in place need to be adjusted, fine-tuned, and optimized before we select and implement software. The plan for how our people will adapt and acclimate to the new processes coming down the pipeline needs to be in place before we select and implement software. Only then will a software implementation truly support our corporate strategy and vision, and only then will it fall within the realm of what we're trying to accomplish – reaching orbit.

While the blueprint illustrates what the overall house or the digital transformation is going to look like, we also need a solid foundation. We don't start framing, flooring, plumbing, or electrical until we've built the foundation. In fact, building a foundation is one of the first things we do when we build a house. The same is true for digital transformation. We need a solid foundation before we start building technology and other aspects of the transformation on top of it.

To build the foundation of a digital transformation project, we need a means of project governance. There needs to be overarching project governance for how we manage vendors, system integrators, consultants, and the project team. We need to have a clear set of processes, roles, and responsibilities, and an overall vision for how the project will be managed. We need to understand the metrics and key performance indicators, or KPIs, associated with our transformation project. We must have a grasp on what defines success.

Aside from project governance, we must also consider our greater technical architecture. We might be deploying a single ERP system, or we might be deploying human capital management, customer relationship management, or supply chain management technology. Whichever path we choose, chances are that we are doing so in the context of other systems that are already being utilized. We have to integrate all systems to function as one, and until we know the current and future, desired state of our architecture, the entire process will be clouded. Our data transfer could be at risk, our cybersecurity could be compromised, and our migration efforts will be tarnished if we don't have a clear view of our web of systems and integration points. These elements will ensure that a digital transformation project will be built on a strong foundation.

Another similarity to draw is that of general contractors. When building a house there is a general contractor that heads up the whole project. That general contractor hires the electricians, the drywall team, the people that do the flooring, plumbing, etc. We also need a 'general contractor' as we begin a digital transformation. We need one party that can manage all the moving parts and stakeholders that are involved in the transformation.

Now, the problem with our industry is that software vendors and system integrators often sell themselves as that general contractor, or they might argue that we don't need the equivalent of a general contractor because they're the ones providing the technology.

That's like a plumber coming in and raising their hand to take on the role of the general contractor.

Most people understand that the plumber is not the general contractor. Those are two very different crafts. The plumber is one of many subcontractors that need to be managed throughout the process of building a home. Even if we're deploying a single type of technology, the software vendor that provides the nuts and bolts of how the software is going to work is just one subcontractor. We also have to address change management. We have to address architecture, data migration, and integration between old and new systems. We have to address the overall program management that ties all the moving parts together.

When building a house, there are very clearly defined roles. The plumber does the plumbing, the electrician does the electrical, and the flooring guy or gal does the flooring. It makes sense because we can see it, we can touch it, we can feel it, and we can tie each aspect back to the blueprint or the architectural work that was done early on.

The problem with digital transformation is that it can be hard to see the different roles that the 'subcontractors' take and the different 'trades' that need to work on the project to get the project to the finish line. Of course, when we talk about subcontractors in this analogy, it doesn't necessarily mean that all the resources we're discussing in regards to a digital transformation necessarily need to be subcontractors. Some could be internal resources. Some could be outside consulting firms. Some of these resources can come from the software vendor or the system integrator. Some multiple parties could provide resources to help with a digital transformation.

However, the key here is to understand what all those pieces are and that it will take more than one party and perspective to drive our digital transformation into orbit. A plumber can't provide an estimate or a blueprint for a new build, nor can a software vendor accurately tell how much time or money it will require to undergo a digital transformation. They're just one subcontractor. They can provide an estimate on the cost and timeline of the software implementation, but not of the rest of the project. When considering a digital transformation, setting the budget, and defining roles, we must make sure to have all those different 'subcontractor' roles defined as it relates to the digital transformation.

Now, in most parts of the world, when a home or building is under construction, there are extensive government regulations on what qualifies as a finished product and what will pass the regulatory compliance measures in place. The problem with digital transformations, on the other hand, is that there are minimal regulations or oversight on how these projects are managed, if any.

If a new build house has a shaky foundation or certain criteria aren't met, then it's not going to pass code and will not achieve approval to move forward until it is fixed. If it's not fixed, the house won't reach completion. A digital transformation, however, does not embody that compliance or verification. The marketplace has no measure of success and stability other than what the company puts forth itself.

We can't rely on the government to tell us how our digital transformation should work. The questions then become how do we validate that we're implementing software the way it should be implemented? What are we doing to mitigate the risk of cost overruns? We must institute similar types of metrics and measurements for our digital transformation on our own.

Our organization must provide the oversight and the verification compliance of how the digital transformation is going. This is a role that independent, third-party consultants can provide. From quality assurance to implementation program management, these consultancies can help provide compliance metrics and milestones that will validate whether or not a project is going to succeed.

When we get creative in our mindset and welcome different perspectives on the black and white practices of software implementation, we will be able to see things in full color. These are general guidelines of how to think about a digital transformation differently, and in a way that most of us can relate to. As you read through the proceeding sections and chapters, consider treating your digital transformation more like building a house.

Before starting a digital transformation, we must be able to answer some questions.

When starting on a digital transformation, people are excited. There is momentum, people are ready to dive in, and it's exhilarating to think about operating at a higher level and increasing revenue. Before we jump in, however, consider answering these ten questions.

Why are we changing?

Oftentimes, organizations think they have a great answer to this question. "We have to upgrade our technology in order to grow" or, "our software vendor is decommissioning an old legacy system and is basically forcing us to move to a new system." Sure, these are good reasons, but it needs to be more comprehensive than 'we have to' or 'we have no choice.'

We must define what our future state is and what we want our organization to be before we dive into the transformation. Dig deeper into this question and find a greater purpose in the project before diving in. We'll discuss how to define our future state in the next chapter.

What business value do we expect?

One way to unpack the *why* is to unpack the business value. These should be elements that influence the performance of our organization. Now is the time to define the business benefits we expect, the impact on supply chain and inventory levels, and what it looks like to improve customer satisfaction.

Once we answer this question, we should quantify the business value in the form of a business case. This is not only to get alignment and approvals on the project, but to set the project governance structure. If we do not set the business value expectations, it will be harder to reach those values.

What is our future state target operating model?

When defining our future target operating model, we should consider what we want to be when we grow up and the target operating model once we get there. It's important to define this future state before we deploy technology.

This target operating model should drive the technology rather than assuming the technology will magically give us the answer of how we want the technology to operate once we go forward. We must define the business blueprint for change and identify how technology will bring that blueprint to life.

What is our future organizational structure?

Just as we need to define our future state target operating model, we also need to define our organizational design. Are we going to restructure? How will technology affect people's jobs? Will certain department tasks become automated, and if so, what will that team do to replace that production time?

As we begin deploying technology, we will get more granular in understanding how peoples' roles will be impacted. However, it's a mistake to avoid the change impact until we are implementing technology. This is an area of focus we need to consider at the beginning to the extent that we can and we can fine-tune the details as we become more ingrained in the implementation.

What type of tech best fits our needs?

Once we have answered the prior questions, we need to consider the type of technology that will help us realize our desired future state. Selecting technology that best fits the future state is critical. We don't want to implement technology that automates things the way we have always done things, we want to focus on automating how we plan to do things in the future state. This is critical if we want to reach our target operating model.

What are the project roles?

Beyond implementation consultants and third party vendors, we need to understand whom within our internal team will be responsible for what. Consider who will be the overall program manager who manages system integrators and consultants, who will be a part of the organizational change management, or OCM, team, who will be responsible for signing off on business processes, and what the roles and responsibilities of the executive steering committee look like. To manage a project effectively, everyone needs to know their roles and responsibilities in order to move the project forward. Our internal team is going to act as the general contractor.

What is our digital strategy and plan?

We need to define our strategy and bring in consultants and vendors to execute upon that strategy. As an organization, we can evaluate the best blueprint and plan that will adhere to our greater company culture, business processes, and system architecture to reach our future state target operating model.

How do we augment the system integrator?

It's important to recognize that our system integrator will not be our silver bullet to success. We not only need our internal team to oversee and lead the project, we also need organizational change management practices and business process improvement that needs to be managed by something other than a system integrator. The system integrator will help with one element of the digital transformation, but they will not be much help in supporting the overall digital and corporate strategy.

Are we aligned?

This is a very important question to ask. Is our team aligned internally when it comes to expectations of the project. Are we aligned around decision-making and project governance, are we aligned on the corporate strategy, and are we aligned on the expectations of the project and the overarching path to reaching our goals? The headwinds of misalignment act as one of the biggest risks of a digital transformation, and it has cost many organizations thousands, if not millions of dollars throughout their digital transformation project.

How will we hold ourselves accountable?

No one person can be the single hand of accountability. Yes, the project rolls up to an executive sponsor, but there are countless other elements that need to be accounted for as well. Other stakeholders need to take ownership in delivering the business values that are expected and that there is minimal operational disruption.

Throughout this book, we are going to walk through the detailed framework needed to outline a winning digital strategy. We will break down the complexities of each pillar that holds up the foundation of the digital strategies of the most efficient and effective organizations. With this information, it will become clear how organizations successfully implement new software, adopt new processes, and keep their teams engaged as they transition from their current state to their future state. It will become clear how organizations reach operational orbit.

By following these tactics, you'll be able to position your company in a way that adapts as new technologies emerge, as markets shift, and as new products and services rise to the brim of the well.

PART I
Processes

Chapter 4
Bridging the Gap

In the fast-paced world that we live in today, it's easy for a company to jump into implementing a new strategy without fully understanding its starting point. Diving straight into the tactics and operations of one's future state without a comprehensive grasp of the existing state will introduce many challenges that would otherwise be avoidable. At a high level, we should think of the future state of our company as the vision. What do we want to be when we grow up? What do we want to be known for? How do we want to operate? What are the differentiators of our processes?

For example, our target future state could be crafted around optimizing our customer service efforts. To get there, we must dial in on our current state of customer service quality and processes and identify areas that can be automated so our customer service representatives make better use of their time. Maybe we aim to have better processes in place pertaining to escalations. If we were to integrate an AI chatbot with conversational capabilities to field the most common customer service inquiries, We would only need customer service representatives for escalations. This would drive efficiencies and eventually save money on payroll. However, we can't just plug in an artificial intelligence tool. We need a thorough understanding of the current customer service practices in order to craft and implement the most efficient and effective plans to optimize our current state. An ideal future strategy in this scenario would alleviate the existing customer service shortfalls. Without understanding the current shortfalls, we won't be able to identify the optimal solutions that would bridge the gap between today and tomorrow's customer service practices.

Too often, the intricacies of a company's current state are overlooked due to the idea that the current state will become obsolete once the new processes and procedures are in place. This false ideation is a pitfall that crushes businesses large and small. We cannot reach point B until we know where point A is, otherwise we are simply floating through space trying to land a rocket with a faulty GPS. It's pivotal that we first understand the ins and outs of our current process. Without a full scope view of our current state, it becomes an overwhelming and daunting task to figure out how to reach our future state. Rather than building processes from scratch as if we were launching a new business, we need to build on what we already have and leverage the clues within our current state processes.

Understanding our company's current state gives us focus and direction. It grounds the greater team in being able to map out how to reach the destination, or the future state. Even if our current state seems broken or inefficient, it's still a starting point. It is nearly impossible to define the future state of an organization unless we can define where we are starting. Asking questions about our priorities, differentiators and unique approach to business will help guide our attention. Asking questions about current processes, current bottlenecks, and the current organizational design will help us create a roadmap that will optimize the priorities, differentiators, and unique characteristics that define our future state. The two perspectives go hand in hand. Performing an organizational assessment to determine these elements before fully flushing out a future state will help us step in the right direction as we formulate a cohesive digital strategy.

A key element to building a sound digital strategy is the concept of proper change management – how to manage change for the people in our organization. It doesn't matter if it's a process change, a change in leadership, a change in technology, or all three. No matter the magnitude or the transformation type, a sound change management strategy will get a team to adopt the new normal with ease. In today's digital era, a transformation in business will almost always be linear with a digital transformation. In the world we live in today, there is no change in business operations without there also being a change in technology. There is no change in business operations without there being a change in the dynamics of a team. There is no change in team dynamics without proper change management.

All efforts to optimize our businesses come down to our processes, and it's the people and technology behind those processes that bring our operations to life. The key is to preserve the processes, technology, and cultural norms that are serving our company in its current state, and work to mold the rest into an improved and ideal self.

Future State

Technology is moving, and it's moving fast. The future of our industries will come quicker than we realize, and it's up to us to keep up. Changes to processes are essentially forced upon businesses if businesses aren't on the offense, continuously evolving with the times. It all comes down to whether the leadership of a company is proactive or reactive. What once were prominent businesses have fallen to the wayside as technology has evolved. Think of Blockbuster, and the evolution of the at-home movie industry. Think of taxis and driving services, and the evolution of the rideshare industry. Businesses, better yet industries, are evolving just as quickly as the technology leveraged within them, and it's those who have a vision who will prosper in this fast-paced world we live in today. Change is the only constant.

We have an opportunity to look at the changing landscapes within our industries and forecast what the future will look like. The key is understanding and redefining our processes to ensure they are robust enough to adapt when changes arise. Change is all around us, and we can either let change control us or be able to appropriately respond to and, thus, control change. By being on top of our processes and continually reevaluating them, we enable ourselves to adapt to changes more quickly. It's important to be disciplined in maintaining a cultural mindset around continuous improvement. Defining our future state with this notion in mind is imperative to staying competitive and keeping our business alive as things evolve.

Leaders often make the mistake of thinking technology will solve the problems of their current state. Maybe there are broken processes or discreet bottlenecks slowing down a production line – those processes and bottlenecks will linger even if they are plugged into computer software. The real solution depends on fully understanding the current state and solving existing problems through prioritizing processes, reworking and redesigning said processes, ensuring buy-in from the people responsible for those processes, and lastly, finding software that will optimize the new processes to the greatest extent possible. That is the only way to a sound future state, and our digital strategy should frame that roadmap.

Going straight to our company's future state under the misguided belief that technology will mend weakness will lead us astray. By incorporating our existing, faulty processes into new technology, we will not only continue to run into the same operational challenges that we had in our current state, but we will also lose our competitive edge. Technology is a tool to help execute on the processes we put in place, but it should never define our processes. We determine our processes. We determine our future state. If we let technology and software determine our workflows and process patterns, then we are essentially squeezing our business into the same cookie-cutter that thousands of other businesses use as well.

On the other end of the sky is the stratosphere, and that is where we will orbit. We are on earth, preparing to launch from our current state to our future state. Our company's future state is ultimately defined as the greater vision for the business, and it is where our operations will fall into orbit. It's where we want to be in five, ten, twenty years. It's our long-term goal in terms of the ever-changing state of technology and how that applies to our present-day business. Without a definitive future state, our company will often find itself lacking direction. The lack, thereof, will lead to challenges when making pivotal decisions, misalignment amongst executives, and, ultimately, the hindrance to the progression and growth of our company's mission.

For our company to define and reach its future state, it will undergo a series of process mapping exercises of both the current state of business and what it will look like in the future. Let's dive into the details on how to clearly define and reach our company's future state and dial in on a premier, competitive, and distinct target operating model for our business.

Target Operating Model

To design and compose an original target operating model that leads to attaining a future state unique to our company, we must take a step back and look at the various elements that play into a cohesive operating model. The biggest inputs are our organizational goals and objectives, processes, and the systems and system architectures in place. These areas will help guide us in crafting our future state and we will break down and optimize each segment to build our target operating model.

Through this assessment, we will build a target operating model upon qualitative and quantitative assessments. Qualitative assessments consist of the analytical findings from the company's current state. Through a proper assessment of our current state, we will recognize what is working and what is not working.

Once all the qualitative information is gathered, we leverage a business process mining software to validate and augment the data to figure out exactly where the breakdown within a given process is happening. Process mining uses data science to identify and optimize workflows. This type of software combines log files from information systems with analytics regarding those processes to make improvements on our current state. Typically, information systems, such as ERP or CRM software, provide an audit trail of processes with their respective log data.

Business process mining utilizes this data to create a process model that displays the end-to-end flow for any given system in detail. It provides insight into whether deviations from the normal operation may be occurring at each point during the workflow. Specialized algorithms can also identify root causes when something goes wrong by automatically tracking changes over time and highlighting areas where problems exist so they're easier to detect than ever before.[2] With this tool, we better understand how workflows are unfolding, how many variations there are in across our many processes, and where the processes slow down or overcompensate. It shines a light on the processes that need improvement.

This makes it easy. When we leverage business process mining tools, we practically have the next steps laid out in front of us. All we have to do is figure out how to optimize the processes that need TLC. By understanding the subpar workflows in our current operating model, we can more seamlessly decide how many employees should be allocated towards certain tasks at one time, how they should do it, and when. Furthermore, it will give us a starting point in painting our vision for the future. We can better determine which processes and operational areas to focus on as we map out our target operating model.

After business process mining is complete, we must ask ourselves a few more questions. Which processes that need TLC are processes that are moving us toward or away from our corporate strategy? Which processes impact the most people in our organization? Which processes are working with our current system architecture, and which ones are the most manual? Performing a high level evaluation of our processes will show us point A, and from there, we need to step into our visionary mindset to determine point B. Point A is our current state, and point B is our future state.

Beyond business process mining and general process evaluations, we also must explore other elements of the organization as well. Defining a future state and building both a corporate and digital strategy around how to reach that point takes a joint effort. It cannot be done by a board, it cannot be done by executives leading from their corner office – it can only be done through the collaboration of all stakeholders. First, we must get ahead of the game by pulling cross-departmental team members together into one room and picking their brains. The people selected should be people who are familiar with the end-to-end processes in consideration of change and evolution toward the future state. After all, a business process mining tool can only tell us so much. It's the people behind the processes and engrained in the workflows that can add color.

Think of this collaboration as a mastermind. Hold a session or a workshop led by an experienced facilitator to dissect what is working and what is not, and discuss which components of the current processes can be improved upon. The facilitator will guide the group toward laying out the steps needed to reach the company's future state based on everyone's input.

Let's talk about a big piece to this puzzle – the facilitator. The individual or individuals chosen to lead these discussions can help document the current state and pinpoint the areas of opportunity holding the organization from operating at a high level. They can ask the right questions that will drill down on necessary process improvements and steer the cross-functional team in the right direction. It's important that the facilitator selected to guide this group is experienced in such a workshop because some employees may find it difficult to think beyond current processes. The right facilitator will inspire ideas and create a safe space for those at the table to voice their concerns with confidence and explore all possible changes that would improve their current operations. Many organizations lean on third-party, independent consultants to facilitate this conversation and optimize the brainstorming process from an objective stance.

As the team goes through this initial brainstorming session and the identification of strengths and weaknesses, it will become easier to paint the picture of what the new normal, or the future state, should entail. The one thing to keep in mind is that even as teams venture into drafting new processes and editing old ones, there may be some colleagues who push back. This can occur at the origination of a new process, or it can occur down the line once the new process is implemented. Regardless of when, it's important that we understand that resistance is a natural part of any transformation. It is often tied to a lack of engagement throughout the planning and implementation phase of a new process. Although we can't fully eliminate resistance as we progress to our future state, we can certainly mitigate it by involving the ideas and concerns of those executing the processes. Not only will this allow for a more cohesive and effective future state vision, but it will decrease the resistance that employees and colleagues experience through the transformation process. We'll discuss resistance more in *Part II*, but it's a concept that should be considered in every instance of strategy formulation and digital transformations in general.

Sure, we can always look to our neighbors and see what processes are working for them, but this comes with inherent risk. By adopting a blanketed copy of another organization's best practices, we are becoming clones of another organization rather than doing something unique and competitive. Identifying the proper approach for our business depends fully on how well we, as leaders, know our current organization and drive alignment regarding our corporate strategy.

It all starts with the corporate strategy – the overarching mission and roadmap of our business. Our digital strategy aligns with our corporate strategy, and it all cascades into the future state of our business. Too often, businesses separate digital strategy and corporate strategy, and they do not speak of the two in the same breath. The misalignment and the lack of connection between the two is what clouds an organization's future state and inhibits progression toward the greater goals and objectives we set for ourselves. Both our corporate and digital strategy should feed into our future state to give us the best chance at attaining it.

With our own unique mission and values guiding us, it becomes apparent why copying other processes will never be in our best interest. Of course, the black and white practices, such as those in accounting and finance that all businesses need to perform are a bit different. In those scenarios, a copy-cat, plug-and-play approach won't be the end of the world. However, it becomes debilitating when forward-facing practices, like customer service and production, take a plug-and-play approach. As a business, we must build and grow on an understanding of who we are and what makes us special. Specifically, we should work with the people on our team that have the expertise around the processes that separate us from our competitors.

Identifying the areas of our business in which we are unique begins with a strategic discussion with leaders and executives about where we land in the marketplace, what our competitors are doing, and the nature of customer feedback. Customer feedback is a particularly critical aspect, which includes understanding why customers are seeking us out and why they continue to return. This is what we must build on. If, rather, we start with a blanketed copy of someone else's best practices, we could be leaving out the things that make our business different and unique, neglecting the very pieces of our business that hold our competitive advantage and attract customers. If we think the cookie-cutter approach is right for us, we must approach it with a strategic eye. For example, consider copying just certain processes, selecting which ones are most critical to our business, and altering them to meet our unique needs.

Another way to lose a competitive edge is to rely fully on technology to help us reach our goals. Rather than relying on a new, shiny ERP software to help us improve our operating model, we first must clearly define our goals and objectives. In this conversation, our goals and objectives are our future state. The clearer the vision for what we want the transformation to be and what we want to be when we grow up, the better outcome we'll have. We're going to find a better solution for our organization if we've defined what we want the future state to look like and have worked backward to map out how to get there. Enter, process improvements.

Once we have fully grasped the peaks and valleys of our current state, we can begin to make changes and improvements. Some changes can be made independently of technology and others can be highlighted as a prioritized need that new technology will need to accommodate. Whichever avenue we choose, it all starts with taking our learnings from our current state evaluations and improving upon them to move the needle closer to our future state.

Chapter 5

Process Improvements

Once a business walks the reflective and visionary journey, they are then able to act. The question is, what should be acted upon? There are countless processes in every business. In order to move forward, we need to pinpoint the processes, or pool of processes, that overlap with our corporate strategy. What facets of the business will move the needle toward the future state?

Well, once we have fully understood our current state and have painted the picture of our future state, we build the bridge out of the processes that carry the most weight. As we consider the different process improvements we should invest our time, energy, and resources into, we must always keep the overarching goals and objectives as our compass.

The process of proper business process management is not only a mouth full, it's a clearly defined path that helps prioritize the elements of the business that will move us forward. Every business wants to drive growth and help the bottom line, but the true corporate strategy will always be rooted in how to do that. Maybe Joe's T-Shirts is planning to drive growth based on the notion that they make the softest, most comfortable t-shirts in all the land. If we were Joe, the processes we would likely want to examine further are in manufacturing and product sourcing. Maybe Annie's TV & Company wants to focus on high quality customer service to encourage customer retention month over month. If we're Annie, the processes we will likely want to examine revolve around all that is front facing. From user interface design to customer escalations, each process should be evaluated from an end to end level to find areas of opportunity. Regardless of the industry, business process management should be an ongoing and integral part of management's role, and it becomes even more important when formulating a digital strategy.

The reality is, if we are involved and engaged in the day to day of a business, then we should have a fairly decent grasp of our organization's current state. We know the high-level, end-to-end processes for the big-ticket items, and we have been managing processes from a top-down approach each day we come into the office. These day-to-day activities make up the core of our company's operations, and all we need to do is look a bit deeper.

To manage a business process is to continually optimize a business process. Many times, a current state analysis will point to a need for the automation of manual processes. More often than not, manual processes are the culprits of common operational bottle necks. By breaking down processes and prioritizing those that are most impactful in driving results, we pour our energy into the big ticket items that keep us aligned with our overarching corporate strategy.

This current state assessment becomes our starting point, and it enables us to build a future state as efficiently as possible through the tweaks and adjustments of our processes. Once we clearly identify the full scope of our current state, we then pave the paths that will lead us to our company's future state operations. This is business process management at its finest, and it's the first step to fully understanding our needs when it comes to finding the software solution that will best help us toward our target operating model.

Depending on the situation, business process management becomes more prevalent at different points along the formation of a digital strategy. However, regardless of the timeline, it will always play a vital role in the success of software implementation and business transformation as a whole. The understanding of our current business processes will help us identify the opportunities for improvement that can be resolved by anything from simple workflow adjustments to robust system automations.

The Roadmap to Business Process Management

Evaluate the Current State Through Process Mapping

The unfortunate reality is that many organizations don't necessarily have the budget, time, or resources to spend redefining business processes. They tend to skip this evaluation phase altogether. However, it is important to review what is working today and where there is room for improvement. As we get started, we should revisit our general corporate strategy. Identify the processes in place that drive the business toward that overarching strategy, and prioritize them as we begin our management and optimization efforts.

First, walk through the processes that are meant to move the needle toward our corporate strategy. Look at them from an end-to-end perspective, and map out the blueprint that outlines the state of the current processes. This is called process mapping.

Process mapping can vary depending on the organization, but at the core, it's a web that outlines our current state processes from beginning to end and the people or positions involved in that workflow. A process map will help identify opportunities for improvement and ways to change how we're doing business. This could include anything from shifting the way we're communicating, to restructuring teams, or to finding opportunities to improve our automation and technology.

A process map might stop us in the middle of a digital transformation initiative and make us reassess the direction we're moving in. It might make us rethink how we're prioritizing processes and help more effectively define the best-fit software through our software selection process. Some organizations may need to get more in-depth in determining what their steps are, while others may find that it's enough to have just a high level framework in order to have people on the same page.

Either way, having a workflow illustrated from where it begins to where it ends is helpful when evaluating where improvements can and should be made. This will allow us to keep what works and change what needs evolution with more accuracy and higher-level awareness. From here, we can move to designing business processes as we see them in the future state.

Design Business Processes

Once we've mapped out all the prioritized processes from end-to-end and understand their workflows, it's time to classify them and put them in the *Hierarchy of Business Processes*. Evaluate each process and categorize them into the two following buckets:

- Core Competencies: These are the things that make us who we are as an organization. It's why we win against the competition, what we do well and what we want to continue to do well. It's our organization's 'secret sauce,' and it usually has to do with aspects of our business that are either customer-facing, employee experience-based, or product-based. It's the things that we tailor and customize to make our organization unique. Without them, we'd lose our edge and our brand would fall flat.

- <u>Commodity Processes:</u> These are things like accounts payable or purchase order processing. It's what all organizations must do, and there are similar processes in place from company to company. These are the processes that don't need customization because they're meant to be generic, and they're efficient being so.

Once the business processes are defined, it's time to drill down even further on existing processes to find the pain points. A pain point can be masked in various ways, and our job is to be cognizant of the different personas those pain points can take. The key is to look for tension and hindrance. Consider the following questions:

- Where is there tension in communication or collaboration?
- Where does the wheel slow down?
- Are there certain tasks within a given process that need to be completed quicker or more efficiently?
- Are there certain data elements that could help someone do their job a bit better than they are currently doing it?

Uncovering the answers to these questions is often done through process mining. The quantitative data from process mining helps us better understand what we can do to improve without losing the unique differentiators that set us apart from our competitors. With that, it's also helpful to understand what other companies are doing that works and does not work.

Define Your Strategy

Sometimes, we must incorporate Once the pain points are recognized and understood, we can go one of two ways. here are two paths we can take.

Path 1. *Evaluate what we could do today to improve existing processes.*

Comb through existing processes. What is working well, and what do we need to fix? Before making any other high-level shifts or changes across the organization, it's critical to fix the fixable prior to implementing any new technology. It's possible that all that needs to be done is an increase in communication, so a weekly status meeting could be beneficial. It may be that there are redundancies that could be shaved down to allow for increased turnaround times. Either way, begin by optimizing operations, and consider technology once operations are optimized. Depending on which pillar the problem process resides, our response could vary. If it's a problem with people, then it's often something that can rarely be resolved with technology. If it's a problem with the process itself or the existing technology, that may be a different story.

Take the example of a team that isn't collaborating. How do we get them to collaborate? Some say implement new technology to enable more seamless communication and workflows. Sure, that's an option, but the reality is that the technology will not be able to alleviate the cultural challenges that sit at the root of the issue. Before shopping for software that could help, we must start with the culture and behavior of the team, department, and even the organization.

Maybe we focus on creating process owners or process centers of excellence. By doing so, we would enable the team to work together in figuring out how end-to-end processes work. Maybe we adjust compensation and the way we measure and reward the team to enable less competition and more collaboration. These elements will move the needle more when the issue stems from a people perspective. Once these preliminary adjustments are made, then we can consider technology tools down the line to help fuel the fire and build momentum in collaborations.

If the problem process is primarily operational, there are a few levers to pull to ensure processes are optimized and clean. Many times, technology can, indeed, serve as a means of optimization in a given operational process. However, until the groundwork is laid out to determine the most seamless end-to-end process, technology won't be as effective as it can be. The processes that are in question of automation should be as clean and lean as possible before pursuing a technology. This means all extra, unnecessary steps should be removed, any redundancies should be consolidated, and the process should be crisp enough to insert into a software. Once our processes are mapped out with intention, it is a good time to consider the technologies that will automate processes and further drive efficiencies.

Sometimes, non-technological investments will drive the greatest results. Whether the problem processes are related to operations or the people on the team, we must start by doing our due diligence. If things work from our initial, non-technological optimizations, then great! If not, consider the Path 2.

Path 2. *Determine the pain points that can be alleviated with software.*

Many times, we can optimize our processes without implementing software. Other times, the only way to optimize a process is by incorporating some level of technology to enable automation. If we get our organization to its most optimized state, as-is, on an operational and people level, then we should consider the third pillar: technology. So long as we shape up and optimize *before* we invest in technology, technology may be the very element keeping us from scaling.

This is where our digital strategies begin to take shape. The whole point of implementing a new enterprise software is to help drive efficiencies. Go back to the prioritized processes that still have underlying pain points or have room for further improvement, even after the initial effort made to optimize. Focus on key competitive differentiators that make our business superior in our industry and take note of which processes could use a more standardized approach and which ones need to remain flexible. Take note of the processes that are of the utmost importance and rank them based on how important they are in achieving the corporate goals and objectives. By doing so, we are making a 'must-have list' to take with us as we begin considering our software options. In Part III, we will uncover the best practices behind software selection and integration. However, there are still key factors that need consideration before getting to that point in our digital strategy.

It all starts with our processes. Processes are the moving parts of the machine that keeps our organization trekking forward. The effectiveness and efficiency to each part either encourages or hinders operational excellence. The goal throughout our business process management initiatives should be to understand the current workflows, identify areas of improvement within those workflows, and design a new workflow that best supports our overarching corporate strategy. Once we feel confident in our business process management, we have the green light to dial in on the key performance indicators that will help us measure success.

Chapter 6

Defining Performance Metrics

Seth Godin once said, "Measurement is fabulous. Unless you're busy measuring what's easy to measure as opposed to what's important." As with anything in life, the value that comes with measuring one's performance is what can and will drive success. Without notable metrics in place, it's easy to get lost. Without notable metrics for tasks that truly move the needle, there will be no progress.

Take a car, for instance. We look at the dashboard, and we see gauges that tell us everything from how fast we are driving to how much gas is left in the tank. We know how hot or cool the temperature of our car is, and we know when it needs an oil change. Would it be helpful to track the weight of the passengers and cargo in the vehicle? Sure, it could provide some useful information about how much energy the car will expend, but it won't make a difference in the grand scheme of our trip from point A to B. A car manufacturer would never replace the fuel gauge with a light that detects whether or not the tail light is intact. Again, these would be helpful pieces of information to know so you can avoid getting a ticket for a tail light outage or using too much energy, but it's not critical to the functionality of the car. If the tail light is out, the car can still drive, but if the gas tank is empty, we're stuck.

The same thought process occurs when defining the metrics we should evaluate regularly throughout our digital transformation. The key question to ask is *are these metrics going to paint a picture of how close we are to our target operating model and our future state?* If not, then we need to deprioritize those metrics and fine tune our measurements to reflect the overarching goals and objectives of the company.

Oftentimes the metrics used in the current state of the business will differ from those used in the future state. The difference is rooted in the fact that there may be data limitations in place in the current state, and it's not a concept that meets the eye quite yet. This could be a factor that drives the implementation of a new software. Some metrics are core operational metrics that will remain constant as we venture from our current to future state. Other metrics are out of reach in the current state and would provide key insights that would catapult an organization into its future state.

Knowing this, the key to defining metrics is defining the ones we actually need. Many times, we know the metrics that are needed to perform at an optimal level, but it's done manually. A sound digital strategy will help automate reporting on the metrics that we need in order to operate at a high level, or at the level of our future state. As we build out digital strategy, it's important to know that as organizations evolve, key performance indicators will evolve as well.

It's hard to argue with numbers, and the right numbers will help shine a light on areas of opportunity. If we, as a team, are not reaching the competitive benchmarks within our industry, we know that pouring into that lagging bucket will help us improve and grow the business. At any point in time, we can dial in on the average inventory carrying cost for a manufacturing organization. Where do we stand in comparison? If we are way off, then we know we are spending too much and we can put new strategies in place to improve upon the existing numbers. As more and more useful data is uncovered, we are able to craft new processes, new management practices, and even entirely new operations to hit targets that will help our organizations evolve into our desired future state.

Most of the time, businesses look at cost reductions and technical debt. On the surface, that's what seems important, and it is indeed important. The problem is that metrics are misconstrued as only numbers to many. Rather, it should be a holistic analysis. Qualitative elements like user adoption or behavior within the organization are also critical metrics that should be measured as well. A sound digital strategy will entail a cocktail of metrics that measure both quantity and quality. It's not just defining our high-level KPI of increasing revenue by 5% per year. Dig deeper.

How can each department within the organization help the company reach its future state? The overarching, big picture metric is the north star, and our digital strategy needs to paint the granular steps we should take to get there. Those steps are what we need to measure. Each metric, each step, and KPI should roll up into our digital strategy, and our digital strategy should roll up into our overarching corporate strategy.

If we begin with our future state, or the end result rooted in our corporate strategy, we can work backward to determine the appropriate metrics we should focus on as an organization. The defined targets will tell us the data we need to collect. If our target is to be number one in customer experience, then our metrics should all pour into how we can optimize customer workflows. This includes front-end and back-end order processing, production lead times, customer satisfaction, etc. Once we determine what to measure, we can then determine how we will collect the data and ultimately draw upon the right software and digital solutions that will automate the processes. At its core, a digital strategy will define *how* to reach our corporate goals and will utilize technology to make it simple, clean and automated.

Peeling back another layer to this discussion, we need to look at exactly how to drive improvement. Say we measured it, and we're off target, whatever *it* is. How exactly do we improve *it*? How do we improve our customer satisfaction survey results? How exactly do we drive topline revenue growth? How do we do a better job at managing our assets? It doesn't just happen because we have the data, we need to go a level deeper pull the story and science out from the data. This is where we analyze all aspects of the data we are collecting in relation to all three pillars of our digital strategy: Processes, people, and technology.

For example, say we come to realize there are gaps and silos between teams and departments. Processes don't flow, there are system limitations in our existing systems, and people who don't work together regularly are not pursuing each other to bridge the gap. People have lost their way in the organization due to a lack of collaboration and communication, and it's starting to show in our production efforts. What do we do?

The first step is to perform an organizational assessment to quantify where we are versus where we need to be. From there, we outline the ways we need to improve, and ultimately, how we can improve. Yes, it's technology and tools, but it's also managing and driving cultural changes, setting expectations, managing people in an empathetic way, and helping employees grow personally. This analysis will birth a change management action plan for the leading indicator of the silos keeping our organization from fully embracing and optimizing any new processes or technology that we implement.

A similar analysis might point to the biggest operational issues present in our warehouse operations, or maybe our manufacturing processes. It may shine a light on bottlenecks in our sales processes or our customer service initiatives. When we look, we shall seek. When we ask, we shall receive. We can't close our minds into a corner thinking we already know what is wrong. Follow the data to get the whole picture, and move forward from there.

At the end of the day, organizations should take time to find the metrics that are meaningful to them and help them quantify their goals. Whatever we measure will grow. Pick measurements that will move operations and production toward an optimal future state. The ability to measure our processes and data will highlight areas of opportunity and point us in the right direction.

Chapter 7

How do Processes Change People and Technology

Changing a process has a ripple effect. That wave rolls through even the most distanced elements of the business, and although a person or technology may be distant from the actual change, they are bound to feel the impact. If we think of our organization as a machine, it becomes clear why even a small optimization in accounting may be felt all the way in sales and marketing. This ripple effect moves through the entire organization, and the level at which it's felt increases in correlation to the size of the change.

If Jill in accounting can operate her accounts receivables in a more efficient way, the company will indirectly be able to optimize cash flow. If cash flow is optimized, there will be more opportunities for last-minute sponsorship at pop-up events to drive sales because there will be money on hand to pay a the sponsorship fee. If funds were tied up, there would be an opportunity cost associated with lost sales from missing the event. There is a connection in every facet of our business. Each process carries weight, and users are connected and dependent on other team members. For that reason, managing change in processes is pivotal to the success of an overall transformation.

Typically, most transformations involve both operational process improvements and technological optimizations. There is a lot of value that we can unlock in those two areas. However, none of that actually happens until we close the circuit with proper organizational change management. Processes affect people in a lot of ways. The most apparent way is the impact on one's day-to-day activities; It's learning how to use a new tool and getting acclimated to new operations. One of the easiest ways to think about the conceptual value of organizational change is to think about the major components of any sort of transformation and how change management fits. Without efficient change management in the middle to connect the dots between operational improvements and technology, the change simply isn't going to happen.

Even when change seems small or incremental, it will always be larger and carry more significant impacts than an organization may think. If the impact of a change in process is underestimated from the start, then the efforts to improve and optimize that process are subject to creating operational disruption. In addition to the impact process changes have on the people of an organization, they also impact technology in a definitive way.

Processes should drive technology, they should drive the design of our systems and construction of our system architecture. There comes inherent conflict when we have a need for a process change that our technology cannot accommodate. This, often, is where an idea is sparked for a company to pursue some form of digital transformation. One of the most concerning setbacks in a business or digital transformation is the material factor. The material factor could be, for example, reallocated work that now sits in the hands of a different department that doesn't have the skills or experience to be successful in managing these new processes. This material threat could funnel into performance disruptions and ultimately translate into a decline in employee morale.

In *Part III: Technology,* we will walk through the delicacies of technology and the considerations for software selection, but it is all born here. The technology we seek should always speak to the processes we create, improve, and replace. The impact of a process change on the organization and its people should be considered when selecting the perfect software solution. As we work through optimizing our processes, we must have clarity on where it's acceptable to water down our processes, customize processes, or bolt-on another application that will help us facilitate reaching our desired future state.

As we'll discuss in Part II, resistance to change should be expected no matter how large or small the change is. The word 'resistance' often sparks a fear that our people will flat out reject the initiative. But 99% of the time, people *want* change. They understand the need, they become excited at the idea of progress and growth. It's the things you can't see that present the greatest problems. Most executives do not anticipate what may be below the surface. People who are on board with a project in the beginning may become subconsciously threatened when the change impact starts to settle in. When the new job functions replace the old, when the old responsibilities fizzle and the free time is unfilled, people come to question their role. They come to question their value when the process they personally created is replaced with a new system. The unintentional resistance to change often reveals itself once everything has gone live and seems to be going well, and it can be an expensive issue to resolve if not addressed up front.

The key to overcoming resistance when it comes to implementing a process change lies in the manner in which it's addressed. It should, first and foremost be understood. What is the root of resistance? If it's a lack of understanding of how to operate the new processes, then we'd use a different approach than if it's a lack of agreement with the need to step away from existing processes. A proper change management strategy that accommodates a shift in processes will be designed and crafted in a way that frames out the benefits of the change. At the end of the day, all humans are seeking progress and growth, and it's up to us as leaders to frame the change as such.

Chapter 8

Next Steps: Perform an Operational Assessment

Now that we've dug through the different elements of the first pillar of our digital strategy, Processes, it's time to build. As you sit in the conference room with a clean slate whiteboard and talk about business processes with your team, utilize the tools at your disposal to help you get started. For example, APQC is a non-profit organization that provides a technology agnostic business process framework for several industries in a few different functions. They provide benchmarks related to your industry processes that you can use as a reference point. There are other resources that can aid you in the same breath, but they only provide a framework.

You and your employees know your business inside and out. Before you start, think about who should be involved in the conversation. Who are the stakeholders that are going to be involved in defining the current state vs. the future state? It is important to make sure that the key stakeholders, such as mid-level management, as well as frontline employees, are involved in these discussions. It's not necessary to include every single person within the organization, but solidifying an effective cross-functional representation will help in the development of future state business processes based on the knowledge they have of the current state.

As we approach next steps, try not to overanalyze business processes. Focus on where the processes depend on people and where they depend on technology. If the evaluation is bumping up against the point where it really depends on the technology and how it's deployed, stop and assess the rest of the details after the technology deployment takes place. At the end of this assessment, you'll have a strong checklist of needs from a prospective technology, you'll develop a clear strategy for how to deploy the technology, and you'll dial down on the change management strategy you'd like to use. These elements will come together to create our overarching digital strategy and the roadmap to a successful digital transformation execution.

Step 1

Assess the current state and map out current processes.

The future state cannot be achieved without understanding the current state. It is about understanding the current business processes, what's working well, and identifying inefficiencies or breaking points throughout our existing processes. The retainable processes can be built on, and any breaks can help target areas that need improvement.

The first thing to when it comes time to map out our processes and perform a gap analysis is to create a *Hierarchy of Business Processes*. As a refresher, it's all about process mapping and prioritizing our processes by placing them within a hierarchy. The hierarchy has five levels, with commodity processes landing at level 1 and core competencies landing at a level 5. After levels 2 and 3 are when the type of technology we leverage starts to matter.

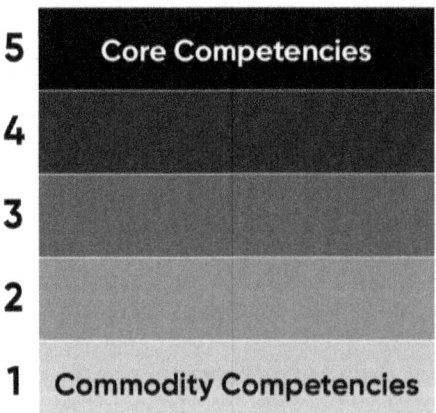

Core Competencies: These are the things that make us who we are as an organization. It's why we win against the competition, what we do well and what we want to continue to do well.
Examples: Processes that are either customer-facing, employee experience-based, or product-based. It's the things that we tailor and customize to make our organization unique. Without them, we'd lose our edge and our brand would fall flat.

Commodity Competencies: These are things like accounts payable or purchase order processing. It's what all organizations must do, and there are similar processes in place from company to company.
Examples: Processes that don't need customization because they're meant to be generic, and they're efficient being so.

Define your core competencies, or the processes that differentiate your organization from competitors. The define your commodity processes, or the processes that are similar from company to company (such as accounts payable, order processing, etc.) Rank each of the processes to help you dial in on the processes that need to be further evaluated.

Do not overanalyze the current state operations down to the transactional level of which buttons get pushed and what fields are entered. A simple, clear overview of an end-to-end business process is enough. Evaluate how the current technologies function, map out existing processes and define people's roles and responsibilities as it relates to those processes to provide valuable

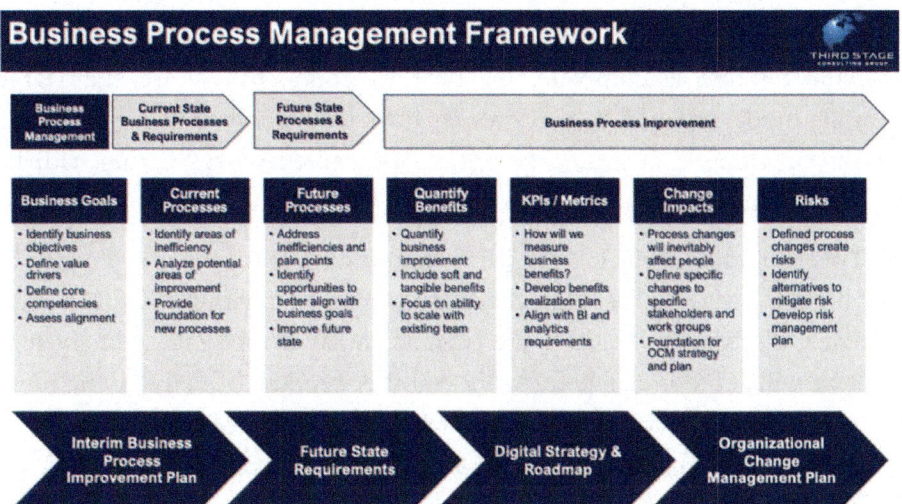

insight that will set the stage for achieving our desired future state of business processes.

Step 2

Incorporate business process mining

Business process mining is a fantastic method to further understand the current state. With this tool, you will be able to not only understand the qualitative conversation around what processes exist, but we'll also discover a quantitative discussion regarding the actual metrics around those business processes. It paints a visual picture of how business processes work in our current state business.

This tool will highlight where processes slow down or show variances. Focus your time and energy on those processes ranked between 3 and 5. With the data you find through process mining, you'll be able to lay down the foundation for a future state based on actionable, focused data.

Step 3

Define the future state.

At this point, the current state has been evaluated, opportunities for improvement and standardization have been identified, and successful processes have been retained.

After all that is complete, it's time to define the future state target operating model and end-to-end process flows that will inch our organization toward our ultimate vision. This is the capstone exercise. Starting with the current state, or as-is processes, and evolving to the future state, to-be process.

This should not only look at what the business processes are going to be, but what the roles and responsibilities are going to be within the future state. Ultimately that's going to drive the organizational change management plan, which we will get to in detail in *Part II*. Another product of defining the future state is a solid set of requirements that will help define, evaluate, and select the best technologies for our organization. These same requirements will also become the foundation for deploying the technology. The upfront work on business process definition for the future state is not only going to ensure our business selects the right software, but also that we deploy the software in a way that enables the right process improvements and supports people along the way.

Step 4

Outline process improvements.

Within the exercise of understanding the current state, you will inevitably identify areas of potential improvement. Bottlenecks will become clear, pain points will find their voice, inefficiencies will be uncovered, manual entry of data will show itself, and quality issues will become apparent. All the issues hindering our business operations will bubble to the surface within the assessment and evaluation of the current state business processes.

Along with the tainted processes, you'll also be able to see the golden processes. Through the initial assessment, processes that are strong and intact will also rise to the surface and show us what is working. These are key parts of the business and operating models that should be retained. These processes are the deal breakers in that replacing these successful processes within the operating model will cause problems. That's why the current state enables you to identify what those future state potential improvements are.

A common exercise that happens in defining future state improvements in the identification of variations in the business processes. If our organization has undergone evolution such as mergers or rapid growth, we likely house a variety of business processes that have been patched together. Let this exercise act as a time to identify opportunities that create a common operating model that will standardize processes to some degree.

Again, this discovery process does not need to be completed for every function and all processes. There may, however, be low-hanging fruits, or areas already targeted for improvement. Always refer to the Hierachy of Business Processes and rank processes on a scale of 1 to 5 to determine their priority level. Focus on the high priority processes that truely align with the company's overarching business strategy.

Standardization will help, but it is important to look at all areas that need to retain a certain amount of flexibility, decentralization, and localization as well. Each business is different. As you go through this step, remember that there is not a one-size-fits-all answer for an entire organization. Consider making only the business process improvements that make the most sense for the desired future state.

With the information and plans garnered from a operational assessment, you will be able to bring everything full circle. These insights will unlock the door to who will be impacted by the changes and to what extent. This will give you a starting point to drafting an organizational change management strategy that would best fit your company culture.

It will also lay the groundwork and a 'must haves list' that will assist in dialing in on a short-list of viable technology solutions. You'll understand process prioritization, the sequence that everything must be rolled out in, what the interim system architecture entails, and business intelligence and reporting needs. Take everything we defined in the assessment and use it as the start of a business roadmap that leads to our optimal future state in today's digital era. This is part one of your implementation plan. Save this, and you will revisit it and comb through it once more toward the end of the book.

PART II
People

Chapter 9

Why Organizational Change Management Matters

"It is not the strongest or the most intelligent who will survive but those who can best manage change."

- Charles Darwin.

This holds true in every aspect of life, regardless of whether it's personal or professional. There's a reason why organizations like Weight Watchers or Alcoholics Anonymous exist. They are, essentially, organizations that help people through personal transformations of their own. They help people manage change and get past the discomfort of finding a new normal using specific goals and processes.

The thought of positive changes initially gets people excited. Maybe it's the thought of finally being able to run a marathon, or being substance-free and living a more fulfilled life. Maybe it's automating our warehouse operations to drive efficiencies in our processes. Whatever the change, it's often perceived with excitement to think about potential improvements at the other side of the finish line. However, when it comes down to it, most people will regress into old habits and revert back into their comfort zone if they are not able to effectively manage change and sustain a new normal. All the effort, time, and money spent trying to improve a situation will be pointless, and in some cases, detrimental, without the right change management strategy.

An organizational change management plan is one of the primary aspects of formulating a sound, overarching digital strategy. As an organization gets ready to undergo a transformation as large as implementing new enterprise technology, it cannot afford to let organizational change management, or OCM, be an afterthought. Many companies make the mistake of neglecting OCM until the middle or end of a project, leading to gaping operational holes once it's time to go live. After all, technology is only a machine until it's powered by people. Without the support, understanding, and buy in of those who power the technology and operate the processes, these high-capital projects may flat line.

Now, why is it that many organizations keep OCM by the wayside until they're deep into the project? It's simple: Misalignment. Many times, those in charge are more focused on capital expenditures and meeting deadlines than they are ensuring their team will successfully adapt. They are simply not aligned on the significance of organizational change management.

Change management is one of the most critical success factors for digital transformation, and yet, it can be very difficult to sell an entire executive team and other key stakeholders on the concept of managing change as a part of a greater digital strategy. This is particularly true with executives and people that don't have a lot of experience with organizational change management, or with complex digital transformations in general. The following key points can help companies attain buy-in from stakeholders and executives and enable their recognition of the need for a strong OCM strategy. If we take these points to the board room with us, we will better acquire buy-in from decision makers to pour into change management just as they do into process management and software implementation.

Define Organizational Change Management

To understand what change management is, it often helps to start with what it's not. Change management is not a soft, intangible concept that will have the team sitting in a circle singing "Kumbaya" and making each other feel good. There is a lot more to change management beyond just training people on how to use the new system or follow a new process. In fact, we can argue that the success or failure of an organization depends entirely on how well the people behind the day-to-day processes acclimate to new terrain.

Organizational change management is about tangible business results. It's about the impact that a given change will have on our employees and team members, and ultimately understanding how individuals and workgroups within our organization are going to be affected. Once we understand what the change impact is and, more specifically, *who* will be impacted, we can craft targeted communications, training, and change efforts to fit the need. To keep

...ganizational change management relates to any aspect of our ...gy that will take our company from where it is today to where it ...n five, ten, maybe twenty years. It will always be people that drive processes and technology. Without people, we simply have a process map and a machine.

Change Management Prevents Failure

During my career, I've had the honor of serving as an expert witness in high-profile lawsuits involving the largest software vendors in the world and entities that lost capital as a result of implementing their well-known software. Believe it or not, there is one common theme across all implementations that go to litigation: A lack of organizational change management. Oftentimes, it helps to share that exact sentiment with stakeholders to help them understand that change management is an absolute driver of success vs. failure. As we discussed at the beginning of this book, there are two common layers that define success versus failure when it comes to a digital transformation.

1. Implementing On-Time and On-Budget

Companies that don't invest appropriately in organizational change management will ultimately find that they will spend more time and more money on their implementation than they would have if they had invested appropriately in organizational change management. Investing time and energy into a strategic organizational change plan is absolutely critical to ensure that we're successful in our implementation.

2. Operational Disruption

The second dimension of failure, which is even more costly and more turbulent than the first, is the concept of operational disruption. This is what happened to Nike. Their operations became compromised, and in turn, they had to deal with chaotic inventory displacement. Organizational change management strategies mitigate risks to ensure that our people, our operations, and our organization are all operating in synergy. Without that synergy, it will be nearly impossible to reach orbit in our future state, target operating model. If our change management plan is strong, then the transition to new processes and technology will be so seamless that it's more of a non-event rather than a massive, chaotic affair.

Change Management Optimizes Business Value

If we shift gears away from preventing failure and focus more on optimizing the investment, then the value in organizational change management will become even more apparent. There's a reason that most organizations don't manifest the full business benefits they expected out of their technology, and nine times out of ten, it's because the people utilizing the new technology are resisting the change. We'll dive into the different types of resistance and how to get around that resistance in the next chapter.

However, before we dive into the premise and the solutions of change resistance, it is important to tie our OCM plan to the business value that will come from implementing the new technology. An elevated or maximized return on investment is one of the most powerful concepts to use when selling the importance of change management to our stakeholders, especially at the executive level. To explain how a return on investment will be maximized by incorporating a change management strategy, paint this picture at the conference table:

Imagine a scenario where every single front-line manager and employee is using the new software in harmony. Everyone is inputting data accurately, referencing the data as needed, and in turn, spending less time trying to solve problems in their day-to-day tasks. By driving those efficiencies for everyone involved, employees have more time to focus on other tasks, they will feel less stressed, and ultimately, bottom-line productivity will increase. As a result, we'll see a direct increase in our return on investment.

Now imagine a scenario where there are a fraction of employees that are not utilizing the software at its full capacity. Maybe they weren't trained properly, maybe they don't think the transformation is necessary, or maybe they are married to an old spreadsheet or process they created to get the job done and they are now having a hard time pivoting away from it. Whatever the reason may be, we have some employees and managers utilizing the software to gather and track data and some employees who do not.

This could lead to holes in the data, inaccurate information being pulled across teams, and functionalities on the new software that are not being utilized as they should be. In this situation, productivity will be bruised as efficiencies are halted as a result of skewed data. There could be multiple streams of data and reporting attributed to the fact that some people are getting numbers from the new software while others are getting information from an offline spreadsheet. *There is no single source of truth in this situation*, and it holds the power to cause operational disruption, delays in the transformation project, and ultimately a loss on our capital investment.

Those scenario comparisons ought to help get people on the change management wagon to some degree or another.

Let's dig into a client case study that demonstrates the importance of change management strategies.

Standardizing Growth: A Global ERP Organizational Change Case Study

This case study explores the journey of a US-based global organization, founded in the 1920s, which successfully implemented a Tier 1 ERP system to consolidate its legacy environments. With revenues exceeding $6 billion and a workforce of over 10,000 employees, the company faced the challenge of aligning its historic siloed business model with its founder's vision and culture. The Third Stage project support played a pivotal role in assessing implementation readiness, guiding cultural transformation, and aligning the change with the corporate strategy, ultimately achieving global data and process standardization.

The featured company is a renowned manufacturer and distributor of food products, fertilizer, and agricultural goods. Established in the 1920s, the organization maintained its commitment to the founder's vision and culture over the decades, resulting in sustained success and significant global expansion. However, as the company grew, it encountered challenges related to operating in siloed environments, managing complex legacy systems, and ensuring consistency across its diverse business divisions. To address these challenges, the company embarked on a transformative journey by implementing a Tier 1 ERP system, aiming to standardize data and processes globally.

Project Initiation and Vendor Selection: To achieve its objective of global standardization, the company initiated the Third Stage project with the support of Deloitte. The project team began by conducting an in-depth analysis of Deloitte's proposed implementation plan, ensuring alignment with the company's specific requirements and strategic goals. After a rigorous evaluation process, the organization selected a suitable Tier 1 ERP system that could meet its complex needs and accommodate its widespread global operations.

Implementation Readiness Assessment: One of the critical early steps in the ERP implementation was to assess the organization's readiness for the change. The project team, in collaboration with Deloitte, conducted a comprehensive analysis of various aspects, including people, technical capabilities, and existing business processes. This readiness assessment allowed the company to identify potential challenges, areas for improvement, and key stakeholders whose support was crucial for a successful implementation.

Guiding Cultural Transformation: Given the company's deep-rooted history and founder's vision, managing cultural transformation was of paramount importance. The project team recognized the significance of preserving the core values while embracing change and innovation. Guided by Deloitte, the company initiated a cultural transformation initiative that focused on communicating the benefits of the ERP implementation, fostering collaboration between different business divisions, and encouraging a positive attitude towards change.

Alignment with Corporate Strategy: The ERP implementation was not just a technological upgrade; it was strategically aligned with the company's broader corporate strategy. The project team worked closely with key stakeholders and leaders to ensure that the implementation of the ERP system supported the company's long-term goals and vision. By aligning the ERP implementation with the corporate strategy, the organization was able to gain executive buy-in and effectively prioritize resources.

Standardizing Processes and Communication: A significant change from the historic siloed business model was the emphasis on global process standardization. The ERP implementation allowed the company to streamline its operations, eliminate redundant processes, and harmonize business practices across different locations. This standardization not only improved operational efficiency but also facilitated better communication and collaboration between business divisions, breaking down barriers that existed in the legacy environment.

Results and Benefits: The successful implementation of the Tier 1 ERP system yielded several positive outcomes for the company:

1. Global Data and Process Standardization: The ERP system enabled the company to achieve consistent data management and process standardization across its diverse global operations, promoting greater transparency and efficiency.

2. Improved Cross-Functional Collaboration: By breaking down silos and aligning communication, the company witnessed improved collaboration and knowledge-sharing among its various business divisions, fostering a more cohesive organizational culture.

3. Enhanced Decision-Making: The availability of real-time data and analytics provided by the ERP system empowered decision-makers with valuable insights, enabling data-driven decision-making at all levels of the organization.

4. Streamlined Operations: The ERP implementation led to streamlined and optimized business processes, reducing operational complexity and costs, and enhancing overall productivity.

Through careful planning, cultural transformation, and alignment with corporate strategy, the company navigated the shift from its historic siloed business model to a more collaborative and streamlined approach. The ERP implementation allowed the organization to enhance efficiency, improve decision-making, and reinforce its founder's vision and culture while positioning itself for sustained growth in the competitive global market.

Change Management Reduces Disarray

One of the intangible benefits of dialing in on a change management plan as part of our digital strategy is the simple fact that it will make our software rollout incredibly easier. It will make it simple to integrate new processes because we'll have alignment and everyone spearheading the change, or a part of the change, is ready to adopt the new day-to-day. No one likes going cold turkey. People need to be eased in. As a leadership team, we need to hold their hands as they walk from one side of the bridge to the other. Creating a plan for how and when to announce the change is coming, how to train accordingly to ensure everyone knows the game-plan, how to get everyone excited, and even fine-tuning everyone's acclimation post-go-live will drive the most seamless and effective digital transformation.

At the end of the day, we're essentially creating an environment within our business that can scale. An organization grows faster than it would otherwise if it has a culture of elasticity and is ready to pivot with the company's processes and technologies. It is critical that a business has a sound organizational change plan in order to tie together all the different components of a digital strategy. Without it, it's difficult to craft a solid foundation for growth. In addition, a comprehensive change plan will also help us navigate the waters of inevitable resistance that we will experience from our team.

No matter what our culture is, how big or small our company is, or how much a software implementation will support our organization's growth, there will always be people who will resist change.

The problem is, it's this group of people reluctant to adopt a new way of doing things that have the power to completely derail a digital transformation's success. So, how can we identify and win over the people who don't want to change?

Chapter 10

Understanding Resistance to Change

Change is the world's only constant. We live in a world that is ever-evolving. Not one thing in life will stay constant through time. Yet, even with that promise, humans still face challenges when it comes to withstanding change. Take Fred, for instance. He's a guy who loves cheeseburgers and milkshakes. Year after year, his wife tells him to opt-in for more vegetables to help him slim down and get healthier. When Fred thinks about it, he gets excited. Who doesn't want to have more energy and feel more confident, why wouldn't I want to be healthy? He's on board for a couple of days, but then Fred drives past his favorite burger joint on his way home from work. He says to himself, "One more burger won't hurt." His wife isn't here to give him a hard time, it will be fine. The next thing you know, he's eating burgers and milkshakes regularly again. It's his habit, it's his feel-good food, it's his comfort zone.

This continues until Fred goes in for his annual check-up and is told by his doctor that he is at risk for a major heart attack, and the only way he'll turn it around is if he adjusts his diet. Things suddenly become more serious for Fred, and he finally cuts down on the cheeseburgers. He realizes that in order to stay alive and be here for the people he loves, he needs to push past the discomfort and build new habits and new likings. For Fred, the decision to adopt a change in his day-to-day is rooted in the deep, psychiatric motivator that his life literally depends on making a change and getting used to a new normal.

It's hard to get behind changing a habit that is easy, familiar, or enjoyable. It's the comfort zone that cripples people in moving forward, and it's the comfort zone that drives resistance to change. Yet, the comfort zone is where a vast majority of the world's population likes to live. People often experience a feeling of comfort in their environment when they are familiar with them. A person's stress level and anxiety levels are relatively low when things feel safe and when there is a sense of control in their activities. To step out of this mindset is a challenge.

The psychological toll that change will bring to those who will endure it is too often an afterthought of those who are leading the change. The irony is that this lack of consideration is oftentimes the leadership team slipping into a comfortable thought of their own that technology and processes will be the silver bullet that solves everything. Sorry to break it to you, but there is no such thing as a silver bullet when it comes to creating a digital strategy.

It's time to shift that paradigm as a leader. It's time to stretch our mindsets. It's time to understand that the concept of change is easier discussed than implemented, and when it comes time for Phil in accounting to change his entire process when running through accounts receivable, there might be pushback. It's as true as the sky is blue. The question is, h*ow much pushback?* Mastering perseverance through resistance to change is what will set apart the good from the great.

To get past resistance to change, we first need to know how to identify resistance. Think of the concept of resistance as the iceberg that brought down the Titanic. Only the tip of the iceberg was apparent to the human eye, but it was the giant mass beneath the surface that cause the most damage and ultimately sunk the ship. Every story of resistance to change mirrors an iceberg.

There will always be a small group of people that express or have expressed resistance, making it apparent to the naked eye. Maybe they're vocal about it to their management team or through a survey, expressing that there is no need for change and everything is functioning well as is. Maybe it's people who have shown resistance to different types of change in the past. Regardless of how it's realized, it's the employees that are intentional and obvious about their resistance to change that are the tip of the iceberg.

The struggle comes when employee resistance is unrealized and unintentional. Let's look back, again, at Fred's story. The thought of change excited him. He wanted to feel good and look good, but when it came down to it, he would revert back to his comfort zone. A parallel story can be told about some of the employees on our team that will undergo a change in their duties, whether it's in their day-to-day processes or the technology implemented in an attempt to streamline their responsibilities within the company. This is unintentional resistance, and it makes up for a vast majority of the resistance to change we will experience through our digital transformation project.

When an organization initially announces a change, excitement is typically at its peak. Nearly everyone will buy into the dream – the promise of more seamless operations, the potential of higher revenues, increased commissions, less busywork, etc. – the possibilities are endless. It creates momentum that gets nearly everyone in the organization excited about what's to come. However, as the implementation progresses, some who were once excited will become threatened. Many times, automating an employee's responsibilities will make them question what their role will look like once the implementation is completed. Questions will begin running through their mind that turn their excitement sour. They'll wonder, *Will I still have a job?*

What about the spreadsheet I made that has been a hub for my team all these years?

Am I going to need to learn a new skill?

Before we know it, their perspective swiftly shifts into a fear mindset that drives resistance. It's these individuals who resist the change more than anyone else. It's those who unintentionally resist that have the power to hinder a digital transformation and deflate the potential of a successful software implementation.

When we begin crafting a digital strategy, it's important to be mindful that these two types of resistance will always present themselves when implementing any type of change. The tip of the iceberg, intentional resistance, is visible to all who pass by. However, the unintentional resistance that lies below the surface is far greater in

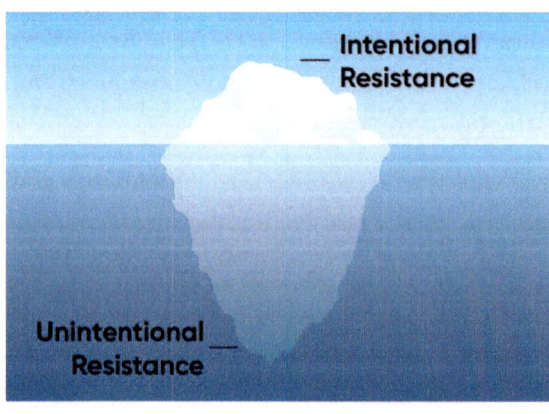

magnitude than what appears to the eye, and it poses a much larger threat to the success of the implementation.

Example of Intentional Resistance

The Head of Sales of an organization decides it's time to implement a CRM that will help his sales team keep track of all their leads and walk new clients through the sales process in an efficient and effective manner. His star salesman, however, is used to simply going to events, networking with prospects, and connecting leads to the business development team via email or text. It's quick and simple, and he's seen great success with it.

During a meeting to discuss the concept of incorporating a new CRM, the salesmen states his hesitations. He believes adding a CRM will only create busy work since he would need to enter in all the lead data rather than just connecting people via email.

Example of Unintentional Resistance

Phil in accounting has a beautiful spreadsheet he created that has helped him track his work for the past few years. He has grown accustomed to entering data on his spreadsheet, he knows where all his numbers are and where to find information, and it's something he was recognized for last year when he took the initiative to create it for his team. It's safe to assume that Phil is going to have a hard time when a new ERP system overhauls his spreadsheet, making his hard work and regular processes irrelevant.

The element that challenges most companies when it comes to improperly managing change is improperly managing the resistance that comes with change. A company can spend millions of dollars implementing new technology, but when the transformation is complete, there will always be a group of employees that becomes proficient at finding workarounds to the new processes in place. They will continue utilizing their tried and true spreadsheets and documents that they utilized prior to the transformation, they will skip the data entry process and just forward information on as they always have. Whatever their comfort zone, they will find a way back to it until they have a reason not to, a reason that deeply motivates them to move forward and stay in that newly produce territory.

There are so many variables that can cause both intentional and unintentional resistance that it makes uncovering the root cause of resistance a seemingly daunting task. However, in order to craft a strategy around how to overcome resistance, we need to understand the root cause of resistance. There are three common root causes of resistance, and once we are aware of them, we can better spot the inherent risk of resistance to change.

Competency

There will always be a fringe group of employees that will serve up intentional resistance. There are two speculative groups that will have the hardest time undergoing a change: The employees who are the most educated and competent, and the employees who are not confident in their abilities to master something new. It's the outliers within an employee base that will often have the hardest time pivoting from their day-to-day, and they will be the most obvious in their pushback to change.

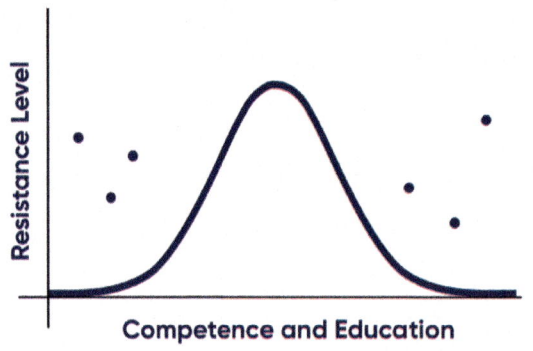

Some of the biggest struggles in change management come with the companies that employ PhD's or highly effective and competent individuals. These individuals have so much faith in the way things work in the current state that they often shy away from adapting to something new. Unintentional resistance will be scattered amongst the rest of the employee base, but this group will typically be vocal.

Misunderstanding

If people do not understand what they are being asked to do or why they are being asked to do it, they will likely resist. When there is not a clearly defined and positioned explanation of what's next, or if there is any fog surrounding *how* the future state will support those who will be losing their sacred spreadsheet, they will likely resist. This is where generic communications can derail a project. We cannot approach a change with a uniform, blanket message to cover every team the same way.

Change affects different departments, functional areas, geographies, and even individuals differently. The communication to each channel should have a cohesive message, but the carrot will likely need to be different for each department. Each department is motivated by something different. For example, those in sales are more money motivated, and those in accounting are more motivated by efficiencies and the decline of 'busy-work'. Having a clear, distinct message that is communicated properly is the first step to tackling any resistance that might come up during a change, if for nothing else, to ensure everyone is on the same page and understand what's happening, when it's happening, and why.

Misalignment

We often talk about how misalignment can destroy implementation efforts. The threat of misalignment also extends into the workforce and the teams that will actually utilize the technology. Often tied with misunderstanding, if a user senses that an upcoming software initiative may impede what they know has worked in the past, resistance will emerge.

Consider the recent case of a consumer goods distributor who was directed by their parent company to implement SAP across all divisions. Prior to this implementation, the small distributor had run a very successful business by creating a niche for their product and maintaining an entrepreneurial spirit in getting things done. It did not take long for users to realize that the procedural mandates that were coming as part of the SAP implementation and standardization efforts of their parent organization would put that entrepreneurial spirit at risk. If things were to become more standardized, then the once flexible and empowering company culture would be compromised to fit the new system that was coming into play.

In this scenario, there was misalignment in not only their understanding of the change but there was misalignment between their culture and their chosen technology. The system they chose did not support their team's entrepreneurial mindset that helped the company thrive and empowered employees to do things in their own way (to a certain degree), and it clashed when it came time to go live with the new software.

The purpose of initially identifying the causes and forms of resistance is to help build a successful organizational change management, or OCM, plan as a part of our greater digital strategy. This is why most change management efforts fail, because most people assume that the same change methodology that worked for one organization will work for another. Each company, each department, each team, and each individual has a varying appetite for change. It is the responsibility of the project leadership and the executives leading the project to be mindful of how the change will impact everything from company culture to specific job roles and responsibilities of those on the team. Once we have a grasp on that insight, we can craft a message that will alleviate the root causes of resistance.

Regardless of the source, it's apparent that intentional and unintentional resistance to change is inevitable no matter the organization. Beyond these initial root causes, resistance can also sprout from cultural issues within the organization as well. Many times, it's the company culture that determines the level of resistance that will play into the organization's push toward change. Some organizations have cultivated a culture of adapting well to change, while others have the opposite reaction. Regardless of where a business falls on the spectrum, gauging the level and rate of resistance we will experience in tandem with our kick-off to any digital transformation is a very important piece of the puzzle. In order to build an organizational change management strategy that will alleviate resistance head-on, it's important to perform an organizational assessment that will highlight the challenges we'll face along the way.

A great place to start an organizational assessment is to send a survey to the greater team. Surveying our team is a critical piece in mapping out our organizational change management strategy. To acquire employee feedback on the current gaps and holes within the current system is to dial in on the true needs of the organization. In every organization, it's a promise that employees have gotten used to current processes and have developed their own approach to completing their daily tasks. To survey our team is to measure their mindset. It's to understand what is going well for them and what is giving them a hard time. It will provide a new lens into the day-to-day of each team's responsibilities. When done correctly, a survey could also shine a light on both intentional and unintentional resistance that will appear once the transformation commences, and it will give us a starting point in building out our organizational change management strategy.

The way the survey is presented is what could differentiate fabricated answers about the gaps in the system and authentic and true answers that reflect the good, the bad, and the ugly that each employee has to deal with each day. Let's face it, if we are going to allocate mass amounts of capital toward a digital transformation project, we want to get a lens into the good, the bad, and the ugly so we can find the right solution. However, if an employee thinks they will personally be judged for their answers, they will not give us the truth. They will only tell us the good, and that's only a part of what we are looking for. Rather, here are a few ways we can induce authentic survey responses from our team.

Have a third-party host and deliver the survey.

This will create a sense of separation between the employee and their company, making them slightly more transparent in their answers. We have to put ourselves in their shoes. Employees will often sugarcoat their answers if they are aware that their management team will review their survey answers. It's far too common that the filtered perspective shared by front-line employees misleads leadership teams to focus on solving the wrong issues. We can't let that happen.

Take management out of the picture and enable a third party to facilitate the survey. If we are planning to undergo a digital transformation, we're likely working with an independent, third-party consultant anyway. It's helpful to lean on them and ask them to facilitate the survey to ensure we are getting the most clear-cut, unfiltered feedback.

Make the survey anonymous.

If employees know their answers cannot be traced back to them specifically, they will be more vocal about their concerns. At the end of the day, we're after their concerns and the areas of improvement. By making known that each employee's response will be anonymous, that is one more wall they will put down while they are delivering their answers.

Ask the right questions.

To set our digital strategy on the right course, it's important to ask all-encompassing questions that will help illustrate the current state of processes. By digging deeper into the specifics, we will be able to identify efficiencies and source bottlenecks in different workflows. We can ask questions like:

- How do you like your current technology?
- How do you feel other department software compares to yours?
- Do you have any spreadsheets that you utilize to complete tasks in your day to day?
- Have you created any specific processes that personally help you or your team succeed?

Throughout the survey, it's also an opportunity to garner feedback regarding our company culture. Include scaled or rating questions that will frame the organization's understanding and perspective of the company culture to help determine the team's appetite for change. Have employees score different attributes of the organization around team dynamics, trust between team members and leadership, and what they believe the company values in their culture.

Once we have this information, not only will we have better insight into the needs of the organization, but we will also shine a light on the tip of the iceberg. We will get a feed for what might come up unintentionally as well. Resistance, both intentional and unintentional, will become fairly apparent after a proper survey is completed. Once the substance below the surface is measured and analyzed, it becomes more intuitive to dial in on an effective organizational change management plan.

Chapter 11

The Power of Company Culture

There are 195 countries across the globe. Each one has its own distinct language or dialect, its own unique cuisine, even its own mannerisms. From the way we greet each other to the way we treat each other, cultures vary from one to the next. There is not one country in the world whose culture completely mirrors that of another. They may try to adopt attributes, but at their core, each culture is and always will be rich in its own unique way.

As we kicked off a new decade in 2020, there were an estimated 214 million companies operating across the globe[2]. The same distinctions that make countries unique are true of companies as well. There is not one company in the world that's culture is the same as the next. There will always be different dynamics of leadership, of collaboration, and of operation that distinguish one company from another.

With this understanding, it makes sense why each company needs a customized organizational change management strategy to help guide a seamless transformation. The reality is that we can only get to where we're going if there is an understanding of where we are today. In this chapter, we're going to walk through how to clearly identify and define what our company culture is and how to mold a culture that can launch a company leaps and bounds ahead of competitors.

The concept of company culture is often undervalued due to its intangibility. Some believe that culture is built on its own through the natural dynamics across and throughout teams. Although this is true, letting a culture grow and establish without any intention behind it is like letting a runaway freight train out the gate. We would be playing the lottery in an attempt to host a positive company culture when there is no strategy or intention behind building one. Once a company culture is established, changing it is like trying

---

2 "Estimated Number of Companies Worldwide from 2000 to 2021", Statista, August 15, 2022, • Global companies 2021 | Statista

to move a twenty-ton boulder – it's not impossible, but it would require special tools and equipment to get the job done.

On the other hand, if we've intentionally built a strong company culture and promoted our core values through every new hire, every team event, and every action we take as a leadership team, it makes a difference. However, the perspective of company culture will vary from a manager or executive to a front-line employee. For that reason, we need to step out of our own perspective and think about how the day-to-day is for Bob in the warehouse or Jill in marketing. Is it the same culture on the sales team as it is in the warehouse? What are the differences and what are the similarities?

What is company culture?

Company culture is often considered the *feel* of a company. It's the intangible element of a business that frames how people feel when they come to work each day. It's the dynamic between team members and between management and employees. Is there an open and honest dynamic between leadership and individual contributors? Do employees trust the management and executive team? Is the team excited about the projects they are working on or do they feel like they need to come to work each day simply to cash out and go home? These are all questions that will help us understand how our existing company culture has been established.

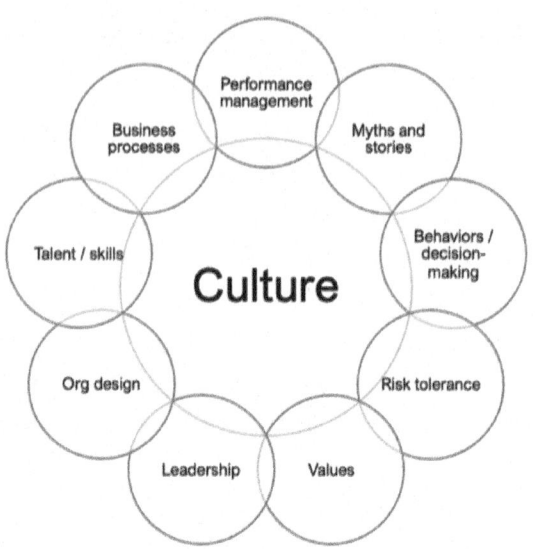

As we begin to ask ourselves these questions as it relates to our specific company, we must look at it from the viewpoint of the various teams that work together throughout the company. Consider these questions from all perspectives to help move the needle in day-to-day operations. The perspective of Bob in the warehouse or Jill in marketing will be different from those sitting in the boardroom, but it's Bob and Jill's perspectives that ultimately form the greater cultural norms of the company. As we formulate our surveys, we must add questions regarding the company's perceived existing culture, otherwise, the viewpoint of those on the front lines could be missed.

The questions sprinkled throughout this chapter are the specific questions we can ask employees via an anonymous survey to gauge how they feel each day when they come to work. As leaders, however, we will need to look under the hood to see what's causing these perspectives. Consider things like incentives, recognition, and the work environment. Are we promoting flexibility and work-from-home options, or does our company value in-person collaboration and host a badging system to make sure people hit their hours? What do we favor as a leadership team, and could it be creating a more political environment than we intend it to? Do we recognize the assist, or only the points scored? How many new employees do we have versus tenured employees? To truly identify and understand the root of our employees' perspectives, we'll need to evaluate these questions thoughtfully and honestly to dissect employee perspectives that serve and harm our company culture.

Besides the fact that having a pulse on our current company culture benefits the greater good of an organization, it's also important to realize that the current culture will either enable a digital transformation or undermine it. Let's take, for example, a company with very siloed operations, no cross-functional synergy, and a sense of competition rather than collaboration from team to team. It would be safe to assume that a transformation would be more of a challenge for such a company than one with an opposing culture. Implementing new software that touches various departments will require those teams to become more collaborative and understand the impacts of their approach on daily tasks. In other words, the company would have to undergo a complete cultural overhaul in order for a new, collaborative digital transformation to work. Without that cultural evaluation and adjustment, a software implementation is at risk of adding little value to the greater organization because it will not be utilized as it should be.

Anytime we begin a digital transformation, an organizational assessment should be performed in order to fully understand our starting point. In the previous section, we discussed how to identify and address resistance to change in an organizational assessment. We will also leverage an organizational assessment to identify and address our company culture, or at least how it's perceived by those working the day-to-day operations.

Let's revisit the reasoning behind bringing a third-party organization to drive authentic and honest feedback from our team. The thought of submitting answers anonymously without having any negative comments tied back to the person submitting them will enable a better feedback loop. It will not only unveil the elements of resistance and determine silos and holes within the organization, but it will also open the door to honest feedback about management and team dynamics. We will be able to weave in questions surrounding the company culture to fully understand and nail down how employees operate on an intangible level in and out of the office. There are a handful of questions we can add to the survey to help dial in on the current company culture.

- Do you trust your managers?
- How would you describe the collaborative culture within your team? How about the greater company?
- Do you feel comfortable asking questions or asking for help when you need it?
- Do you feel comfortable reaching out to others in a different department to collaborate on new ideas? If not, what's holding you back?
- Is there open communication amongst your team?
- What are you excited about within your role at the company?

There are also questions that we can consider as a management team. For example, is the team made up of people who have been there for a long time? If so, this may cause some obstacles when creating change. Or, how can we build trust between leadership and employees? An assessment will uncover the gaps that could come up during a transformation. Without a thorough organizational assessment, we will struggle to understand the current company culture and may hinder the team's ability to transition to a new technology. At the end of the day, our goal in formulating a sound digital strategy is to tie in all the components of processes, people, and technology. It's mission critical to understand the essence of both the culture of the organization and and the essence of the software.

To illustrate the importance of tying the three pillars together, let's take a closer look at the role company culture can play in a digital strategy with the following example.

Final Countdown Case Study Video

The best example of effectively implementing the people, process, and technology work streams, along with the strategy work streams we discuss in the book, is a large steel manufacturer that has been my client for quite some time. They underwent a global transformation, which involved implementing ERP software and other technologies over multiple years across their international operations.

Throughout this implementation, they exemplified the pillars we emphasize in the book. Starting with the people aspect, they managed it exceptionally well, which I believe was the primary reason for their successful transformation. It's worth noting that they have an aversion to the term "change management" and the concept often associated with it. However, they were highly effective in managing change, which is somewhat ironic considering their culture.

In this case, their effectiveness stemmed from their strong organizational alignment and clear set of values.

When encountering different individuals, leaders, and frontline employees across the organization, there is a consistent sense that they belong to the same company. However, it is challenging to articulate and grasp the exact meaning and reasons behind this strong cultural alignment. Nevertheless, it is evident that they possess a unified culture. The leadership team works cohesively towards shared objectives and goals, maintaining a clear sense of their identity and aspirations while also understanding what they do not wish to become. This clarity of direction and alignment permeates the entire organization.

This backdrop of a well-aligned organization served as a foundation for their transformation. Having such alignment is immensely powerful, as many organizations struggle with varying degrees of misalignment. Misdirection creates headwinds that hinder progress, whereas alignment generates tailwinds that facilitate success. Therefore, addressing alignment issues early on is crucial for organizations embarking on transformation journeys.

The effectiveness of their people-centric approach played a vital role in their success. This organization also prioritized the impact of technology on people's jobs. They made efforts to clearly communicate how job roles would change and evolve. Additionally, they effectively integrated technology training with business process and operational training. Taking an active role in leading the training themselves allowed them to incorporate the organization's operational nuances, language, and terminology, making it more relatable and meaningful for the employees. These examples demonstrate their dedication to addressing the people side of the transformation.

On the process side, they displayed strong alignment regarding their current and future business processes. This alignment provided them with a clear direction in terms of which technologies would or would not be suitable for their business. They allowed their business operations to dictate the deployment of technology, avoiding the common mistake of focusing on technology first and attempting to fit processes later. Their roadmap and blueprint for operational goals guided their technology deployment decisions, ensuring alignment between technology and processes.

Speaking of technology, they excelled in managing the technology work stream or pillar. They avoided being swayed by emerging technologies and enticing features that may not have been suitable or aligned with their organization's readiness. Instead, they focused on deploying technology that could genuinely enhance and improve their operations based on their specific needs and goals. They remained highly focused on the desired outcomes of the transformation, steering clear of distractions and unnecessary embellishments that did not align with their objectives.

The organization showcased excellent management of the technology work stream. During their multi-year journey, their software vendor transitioned their flagship product to the cloud. However, the client decided to implement an on-premises version of the technology. Despite the software vendor's attempts to persuade them to switch to the cloud solution, the client conducted a thorough evaluation and determined that the cloud version was not mature enough and did not meet their needs. They opted to stick with the older, more mature version of the software, which proved to be a better fit for their requirements.

Additionally, they displayed effective management of their system integrator, which ties both to technology and the people side of the transformation. They took charge of managing the system integrator rather than being managed by them. This approach, although seemingly common sense, is often overlooked by many organizations who rely too heavily on the expertise of the integrator. By maintaining control and ownership of their technology deployment decisions, they avoided potential pitfalls.

Furthermore, they deliberately slowed down the pace of the project, extending the timeline and reducing the staffing of their technical implementer. This bold move allowed them to ensure that changes were adopted effectively and aligned with their preferred tempo. It demonstrated their commitment to prioritizing their business needs over external interests, such as maximizing revenue for the technical implementer.

Regarding Third Stage's role in assisting the client, it is worth noting that the client was highly knowledgeable and technically savvy. They were selective in their use of consultants and openly admitted their aversion to them. Consequently, the project did not become a massive endeavor for Third Stage in terms of revenue generation. However, the collaboration with the client was valued, and despite their dislike for consultants, they appreciated the assistance provided by Third Stage due to our technology agnostic and independent position in the marketplace.

We played various roles in advising them throughout the project, starting with validating their vendor selection and assisting in negotiations. During the implementation, we provided support in change management, even though they preferred not to use that term. We helped them redefine and redesign their IT organization, aligning it with their future state. Additionally, we assisted them in implementing business intelligence to consolidate information across the enterprise, considering the presence of legacy systems from different vendors.

Furthermore, we offered project management advisory services to ensure the project stayed on track. It is worth mentioning that they maintained control of the project and did not outsource the entire implementation to us, which aligns with our approach of finding the right balance between external support and internal staff involvement.

Our role as an independent advisor and technology agnostic entity was crucial in this project. Their skepticism of external parties and their preference for making decisions based on their best interests necessitated an independent perspective. Moreover, with multiple software vendors involved, potential conflicts and turf wars could arise. As an independent advisor, we navigated these challenges, ensuring alignment with the client's business needs rather than succumbing to vendor interests. The impact and influence of vendors and implementers on projects can be significant, underscoring the importance of having an unbiased advisor throughout the implementation process.

This example demonstrates how the intentional synergy of people, process, and technical required to achieve a successful digital transformation.

Addressing existing flaws to create a more sound foundation for a big shift in company dynamics will help ease the transition to a future state. Let's talk about how to change or adjust our culture, and what it means to do so.

Cultural Change Dynamics

When organizations go through a digital transformation, they typically are also transforming their culture. Now, what exactly is cultural change and how do we enable it? Cultural change is often a key component of any sort of transformation, whether we're talking about a business transformation, digital transformation, or even process changes alone. All elements of change are linked to a change in cultural dynamics and it's important to be mindful of that as tides shift. Oftentimes, organizations are using technology and business processes to fuel and to bend their culture in a way that meets the future strategic objectives of the organization. Let's take a deep dive into the components of cultural change, and how we enable change in a way that compliments the overarching business strategy.

The first step in any sort of cultural transformation is to define the mindset that we want the organization to represent in the future. For example, typically organizations start out small and become larger over time. During that journey of growth and maturing, the organizational culture must evolve to meet the new needs of the business. The culture itself needs to transition and shift and bend to keep up with the changes of the organization.

Let's take a large organization, for instance, that found its success by encouraging an entrepreneurial mindset across the company. As they scale and hit new milestones as an organization, they may find that they need to start adopting more corporate, structured tendencies to keep things efficient and optimize their operations. By standardizing processes and driving those specific efficiencies, the organization is going to inevitably experience a shift in their cultural mindset. The team will pivot from that entrepreneurial environment to more of a structured, predictable environment.

At the end of the day, this sort of shift isn't going to happen overnight, nor should it. However, it can, and should, be top of mind. Start thinking about ways to deliberately bend the culture to migrate in the given direction that resembles the future state and what we want the company to be in five to ten years. As other parts of the transformation are enabled, such as process improvements or technology enablement, the culture will also be a means of further fueling and enabling those changes that we envision.

Other examples of potential cultural mindset shifts that may apply during a transformation may include driving innovation within our organization, fueling better collaboration, greater transparency and better data-driven decision-making. These are all cultural nuances that need to be deliberate and planned as part of our cultural change strategy, otherwise, they will not be achieved. We either steer the ship or the tide will take us somewhere we didn't plan to go.

Business Process Changes

The second part of any sort of cultural transformation is the business process changes or improvements. As we're thinking about what types of business process improvements our company needs in regards to transformation, we should also be thinking about the way that those changes in the workflow may affect company culture. We could even consider the inverse, framing the question around how our company culture can be the very thing that drives or encourages process improvements.

Whatever angle we look at it from, think about our business process adjustments through a cultural lens. At the core, business processes can either become more standardized or more flexible. Some organizations will find that earlier in their lifecycle, a certain amount of flexibility is important. Then, as they scale, standardization begins to trump that which came before it. However, in some cases, a company can become so big, and so standardized, that they find that they need more flexibility again. The cycle continues, and every organization falls at a different point on that spectrum.

As we start thinking about the attributes of business processes discussed in Part I of this book, we're going to find our organization leaning either toward integrating more flexibility, more standardization, or maybe adopting a hybrid of the two. As we design said processes, we can dig deep into how each scenario would affect our company's culture. Is there a way to bend the existing culture to support whatever process improvements we're driving towards? If so, do it.

General Organizational Competencies

Another great aspect of cultural change is the general organizational competency a company has. As a company grows, evolves, enters new markets, takes on new customers, and brings on new employees, the need for different organizational capabilities and skills will also grow. When we think about the company culture, we have to think about what kind of skills and competencies are needed and just how we can construct a successful culture around those new competencies.

We often find that organizations that are trying to use technology to enable better decision-making or better business processes will find that they need new skill sets within their IT organization (we'll dive deeper into this in Part III). We also have situations where a customer-driven focus of an organization may require new customer service skill sets, processes, and technologies to support that. This all requires organizational design, hiring, and recruiting processes that support that entire organizational shift. When we're thinking about our culture, we need to be thinking about those competencies and capabilities that already exist. With that, what is it we need going forward to pivot the culture in the right direction?

Changing Company Culture

We now need to look at this from the lens of processes, people, and technology. We can begin by pondering the question of which technologies will support the type of culture we're trying to create. Often, we fail to consider the impact software can have on a company's culture simply because the two seem distant at first glance. It's easy to let technology do what it does best – sort, organize, and deliver data – without considering the larger cultural implications.

The reality is that technology holds tremendous power in shifting a company's culture, for better or for worse. Assuming that we want to be intentional about our company cultures, it's important that we consider how our business processes will touch the company's culture and the greater team dynamic. If we are an entrepreneurial company but opt-in for standardized processes, our entrepreneurial light will be dimmed. If we have a very structured organization dedicated to a plug and play approach, then implementing a system with flexible modules and ever-evolving processes will skew our day to day.

With that in mind, it all starts with an assessment of our company culture. Dig into the people side of the existing process and technology trifecta. This is where we will find the right messaging and communications, training, and organizational design that will support our digital transformation launch. More specifically, we will understand how to support collaboration, identify talent needs, further build on our strengths, and tend to our weaknesses as an entity. Where are we today in the sense of our employee dynamic? Do employees feel comfortable sharing new ideas with their leadership? What do we value in our organization and how is that recognized when employees embrace those values? Ask the difficult questions that will help gauge the organization's current culture in its current state. If we can grasp our company culture on a scientific level before any changes are made, we have a better chance of leading that change in an effective and efficient manner.

The goal is to view cultural change through various lenses. This will ensure that cultural change permeates everything we do throughout the rest of our transformation. Once we know where we are, we can begin to craft where we are going. What do we want our future state to look like, specifically when it comes to culture?

At a high level, our future state is ultimately what we want to be when we grow up. It's the detailed vision leadership has in mind when they picture the company in five to ten years. As we define what we want to be when we grow up, from a cultural perspective, it's important to also consider how we are going to get there. Depending on how we bend our company culture walking into a transformation, we can inch ourselves from where we are today to where we want to be down the line. Again, it's not as simple as just putting in new processes and new technology and hoping for the best. We need to be more deliberate about the direction we are steering the ship. This requires us to be intricately intentional about change management efforts and understand how each element of the greater transformation will create a cultural change.

Once we are able to piece together a cultural roadmap as part of our overall organizational change plan, we can move on to the next step. Without the cultural and organizational intention behind a business and digital transformation, the project will be moving without a targeted destination. It would be as if we're on a trip headed to Spain rather than to Barcelona, Spain. Without that pinpointed target, we may end up in Madrid or even in the middle of the Mediterranean Sea. We must be intentional and specific about our final destination in order to see the magic unfold as we begin our journey toward orbit.

Chapter 12

Organizational Alignment

Organizational change management is far too often an afterthought. That mindset breeds delays in implementation, budget overruns, and operational disruption – also known as ERP failure.

This mindset is particularly prominent with executives and leaders that simply lack experience in organizational change management or complex business transformations. It's not every day that we are overhauling an entire ERP system and replacing it with a technology that will inevitably push new processes and new organizational structures. The truth is unless we have successfully completed multiple business, operational, or digital transformations, it's hard to grasp what drives success for each unique organization. The landscape is so different from company to company that the overarching strategy must be exclusive to each respective organization.

That exclusivity in company persona is what requires a crystal clear sense of alignment across an organization. We see it more often than not, and it all starts at the top. Executive misalignment is ever more prevalent in today's business environment. While a company could potentially survive for years with some degree of misalignment at the top, the risk increases with each strategic initiative, such as a digital transformation. These initiatives put strain on every nerve of an organization, making executive alignment a critical part of any successful digital strategy.

Now, what does misalignment really mean when it comes to digital strategy? Misalignment can occur on a number of levels: between divisions, between regions, between departments, and across the hierarchical layers of an organization. If the leadership of an organization is marching in unison, then it is possible to fix any of these forms of misalignment. It's specifically when leadership is out of sync when a company will live in a state of misalignment. When the captains of the ship are intrigued by even slightly different treasures, the direction to the crew will be clouded with a fog of uncertainty.

Sure, this executive misalignment can live in day-to-day operations, but it's when processes, technology, and people are put under stress that the weakness will show. This weakness has the power to derail business and digital transformations, throw off strategic investments, and even cause a hostile work environment. The tricky part is that executive misalignment can come in many shapes and sizes and it's often hard to identify when looking at it internally. It's the subtle differences between leaders that drive colossal impact in a company's direction.

In order to compile a strong digital strategy, we must address misalignment at an executive level, at the root. As we explore the nuances and silos creeping in the background of our board meetings, make sure to look at the concept through an aerial lens. This misalignment can be hiding between different executives, between executives and the overarching business strategy, or even in the unconscious and conscious biases each person sitting at the table holds true. Regardless of what shape the misalignment takes, it's important we keep the following red flags top of mind at *every* digital transformation meeting.

Red Flags That Point to Misalignment

A lack of clear-cut governance processes guiding the transformation.

If our company has an 'open door' policy but employees are unsure where to funnel a question or concern, then employees will decide for themselves whose door they want to knock on. When given the opportunity to choose, employees will likely reach out to the executive that allows the most flexibility, even if that executive is not the most qualified to address the issue. This scenario also poses the potential of getting different responses depending on which executive is asked.

Imagine that during a software implementation, a department identifies a critical need for new functionality and wants to purchase a different system to handle their needs in the interim. This type of decision should follow a prescribed process with a clear and distinct sequence of actions. The steps a department or employee should take when purchasing and implementing a new software program should be specific and consistent. If direction is vague and users are instructed to go "ask the executive team" in general, there can be two different responses. The COO, for example, may immediately state, "Yes, we cannot hinder operations." The CFO may say, "Absolutely not, we have a fixed budget that this does not fit in." Where do you think the process owner will go?

Leaders' financial interests are imbalanced during the transformation

Take the previous example. Let's say in this case, however, that the COO is designated as the executive sponsor responsible for approving customizations and disparate products. He is also guaranteed a $10,000 bonus if the implementation is delivered on-budget. In this case, the COO will be incentivized to deny any modifications to the budget, regardless of the potential benefit to the organization. Even though this approach may be based on good intentions, it is a recipe for ERP failure.

Executive technology bias in influencing the transformation

Executives are placed in leadership roles because they have 'been there' and 'done that'. In many instances, their past experiences include ERP implementation or a digital transformation. Often times, if an executive leader had a bad experience with a specific technology in the past, they will carry that bias against the same technology products in the future. They can either veto the pursuit of a system that would otherwise be the best fit for their new organization, or they could bring a heavy load of negative energy to the project. On the other hand, if they had a good experience, they might assume it will all go without a hitch without realizing they may have been one of the lucky ones. Some of the worst ERP failures were due to leaders making a decision to purchase a technology platform simply because it worked in their previous organization.

Undefined corporate strategy

Ultimately, all companies are in business for a reason. Whether they are out to maximize shareholder profit or make the world a better place, their mission was hopefully clearly defined from the start. Following this mission is the basic strategy needed to accomplish established company goals and objectives. If this stated strategy is missing or not clearly defined, then executives will fill in the blanks on their own, resulting in each executive focusing on relevant, yet different, strategies.

Without a defined, overarching mission, a digital transformation initiative will be subjected to the various perspectives of this misaligned executive team. One leader may be targeting simply to replace outdated technology with little disruption, another may be looking to reduce waste, expenses, and headcount, another may be looking to enable growth while another to enable use of data and emerging technologies. Two plus two equals four, but so does three plus one. There are different strategies to get to the same place, and that could be the very cause of the silos between executives. An executive team pursuing different approaches to solve the same problem has the power to derail a project, keeping an organization from arriving at its final destination at all.

These high level examples of misalignment will trickle down as mixed messages to the greater team. When it comes time to execute an organizational change management strategy and communicate the changes coming down the pipeline, a company will struggle without synergy from above. With that said, before we get to the point of mapping out our communication plans and training formats, we need to nip any misalignment in the bud from the very start.

The first step is accepting misalignment. Interestingly enough, executive teams rarely believe they are misaligned. It is often middle management that feels the push and pull, identifying issues and concerns at the top of the organization. The problem with this is that mid-level managers are rarely given an opportunity to share their perspectives. If they do, they may not be taken seriously, and in some cases, they're given a pink slip when they share their views on issues related to the executive leadership.

The smartest way to handle apparent executive misalignment, or even assess if there is executive misalignment, is to outsource. Do not perform this exercise internally. Tap on a trusted consultant that will be able to help gauge this level of understanding and shine a light on potential misalignment issues without having to navigate difficult internal biases and egos. Hiring an objective third party can help smooth the edges of a potentially jagged situation.

Whatever we do, it should be our goal to ensure clear alignment across all aspects of our organizations. We must move forward as one, unified front if we hope to reach orbit. Any opposing or adjacent winds will deter our progress and result in our launch being off target. From the moment we begin discussing digital transformation goals to long after go-live, we should commit to being intentional about minimizing gaps, curbing silos, and bringing all stakeholders together as one.

Chapter 13

Organizational Structure

How do we know what works? More importantly, how do we make sure we keep what's working? It is apparent in our company data and procedures what is not working and what is ultimately hindering operational efficiencies. It is often easier to recognize the trouble spots with our teams and our procedures simply because flaws stick out like a sore thumb. However, in an age of shifting business models, rapidly evolving technology, and shifts in market and consumer habits, figuring out what is going right with our team may be one of the tougher challenges we face.

Let's drill down into organizational structure and how it plays into building a sound digital strategy. Think of an effective organizational structure as a snowball rolling down a hill. Yes, the snowball will continue to grow larger as it descends the slope, but that's not our focus. Our focus should be on the snow that doesn't quite latch on, enabling the snowball to form into a round, smooth ball of ice as it picks up speed. Some snow just isn't meant to become a true part of the whole, even if that snow sits in the path of the descending snowball. The snowball will fling away pieces that don't fit into place and will pick up the freshest powder to mold into its surface. Organizational structure should be addressed like this snowball. One can only get the cleanest, strongest, best end result when the organizational structure is molded using only the pieces that fit best.

Let's take a look at an accounting team that's been successfully cranking out deliverables for their company for a fair number of years. They hum along with minimal oversight because they've become a cohesive, goal-oriented, and progressive team. Even so, change lingers. A new artificial intelligence (AI) technology has been introduced to their CFO, and the leadership team knows the same work can be done much faster and more efficiently if the AI technology is integrated into the mix.

What has made the accounting team successful thus far is that each member relishes their role and has been excelling at what they do. However, they are now facing structural change rooted in the overhaul of their day-to-day practices. In order to modernize and prepare for new projects to come, the executive team agrees to integrate this new technology into the accounting team's operations.

Right out of the gate, the team discovers that digital means something different today than it did five or six years ago. Machine learning and AI have grown as tools in the organizational toolbox, pushing their way into the realm of business intelligence (BI). The accounting team has been tasked to get trained and become well versed on the new AI system immediately.

By nature, this shift in operations will shift the accounting team's organizational structure. The AI system is added to the team's skill set, but it is automating many parts of team members' roles. Phil in accounting may have been the point person to process accounts receivables, but that entire task is now automated. What does that mean for Phil? What will that mean for Phil's management team? Will Phil be a spec of snow that is flung off the greater, rolling snowball, or is there still a place for him with redefined responsibility?

While building our digital strategy, this restructuring of roles and responsibilities should play into our thought process. Once we implement new technology, what will that do to our organizational structure? We need to think about which roles will be impacted, and more importantly, *how* those roles will be impacted. The natural fear that drives resistance to change is entrenched in the thought of losing what one has. In order to mitigate resistance, we must think about this scenario in advance and manage the expectations around it.

Maybe it's a message to the greater team that although job functions may shift, there will be new opportunities for everyone impacted. We could reassure the team that there will be no layoffs, or that if there will be changes in team structure, there are resources available to grow one's skill sets and adjust to the needed changes.

As leaders, we need to be comfortable with the idea that it's okay for things within our organizational structure to change as long as we approach it with empathy and intention. If it works and the snowball rolls faster and smoother as it grows, that's just fine, so long as it continues to roll in the right direction. The parts that aren't working effectively will be shed along the way and used to water the grass beneath it.

Let's take another example of a company that has scaled through multiple acquisitions, consistently buying up smaller competitors with similar services. This company has expanded dramatically and has kept each acquired entity operating fairly effectively as it holds onto its original processes and technologies.

Although the business continues to function, the independent systems and cultures that have come with each company acquisition have created silos. There are culture gaps, and even process gaps between departments within this ever-growing company. After some time, the company begins to feel the weight of the various processes, technologies, and cultures under one roof. The snowball rolls downhill, but it labors now. There's not as much inertia, not as much good energy, and many bumps that slow it down along its path. Rather, there is wasted effort and the company may only be able to sustain its size for so long. The only way the company can function optimally is if the various departments find synergy.

Finally, the COO decides to transform the disparate parts into a single unit, crafting a digital strategy that will ultimately bring the entire organization onto one software platform. By doing so, common grounds of practices and communication will be born. The move will reverberate all the way down to new roles and responsibilities amongst managers and peers. There will be new team-to-team collaborations, there will be teams and departments that consolidate efforts under one leader, there will be new roles and positions created, and some existing roles will be redefined. This level of change will drive a shift in the foundation of the organization's structure.

It's imperative that the leaders of this organization think through the new structure clearly before moving forward in selecting software or adjusting processes. Of course, the final organizational structure will shift through the digital transformation, but it's important to walk into a project with a vision of what that new structure could look like.

To keep the company moving forward efficiently is to keep the snowball rolling. This brings us back to figuring out what is right with our company and enhancing the synergies and processes that enable us to succeed. Our digital strategy should be integrated into the forefront of our business, as it affects every element of a company. Most importantly, it impacts people, and it will enable our organization to operate in its most efficient state. Many times, it's the emerging technologies of the world that will push our organizations to perform optimally, but our perspectives will vary depending on which side of the table we sit.

Employees, more often than not, are the ones that jump to the big question of the twenty-first century: *Will robots take my job?* It's not as far-fetched as some might think. Honestly, it's not far-fetched at all. A company might need to integrate new technologies to stay relevant in the marketplace, and that will inherently shift its organizational structure to better incorporate components, such as AI, in order to keep at the top of its game.

The reality is, many existing jobs can and will be automated. Whether it be by robotics process automation, AI, or any other emerging technology that has yet to be developed. It's inevitable. However, what will come of it will be far greater. New roles and responsibilities will be born as a by-product of advancing our technologies. It was in the 1970's and 1980's when society feared computers. People thought the world was going to be taken over by computers and that their jobs (punching numbers into a calculator and crunching numbers with a pen and paper) were done for. They thought their careers would be gone and their livelihood destroyed. But, what actually happened?

The profession of information technology was created. Universities began teaching students how to develop, how to code, the ins and outs of process automation. Newer, higher-paying jobs in technology filled the market. Those who ran the numbers with a pen and paper or managed files began to do the same, just in a cleaner, more efficient way. It was quite the opposite of peoples' initial fear that occurred. Rather than losing their jobs to computers, they got better jobs managing the computers. The shift pushed society forward, pushed the human mind to higher levels in understanding, and ultimately enabled us to get much more done as a species than we could have before.

The same will be true for artificial intelligence, robotics process automation, and all other emerging technologies that are currently viewed as a 'threat'. Sure, many roles and job duties will indeed become automated, and maybe the need for a person on the packaging assembly line will dwindle. However, with it will come the opportunity to learn how to operate, maintain and optimize the robot that will now package the products on the assembly line. The only element that leaders and developers alike need to be mindful of is putting good people in charge of the technologies that will soon dominate the marketplace. Technology will always be submissive to the people managing, maintaining, and developing it. The power will sit with the people that know how to operate technology. Whomever we select to sit in that chair, we must make sure we trust and support them in their approach.

A leader within an organization shifting to new technologies must strategize and communicate what the new organizational structure will look like. Team members will inevitably get bumped from their existing roles into a new role as a result of a robotics process automation or an AI integration. Maybe there are advantages to taking someone off the accounts payable focus and putting them into a role where they can assist the team's new system. Either way, having a smoothly operating organizational structure will help a business with the following:

- Quicker decision-making
- Improved operating efficiency
- Enhanced employee performance
- Decreased duplication of work
- Less employee conflict
- Better communication

Our company will inevitably diversify its goals and perhaps even its products or services, and the organizational structure will change, then change again, and then change yet again. Our change management strategy should focus on this, as should our organizational structure and our ERP systems. A focused, synergetic digital strategy helps us weave all these facets together, like a solid, smooth snowball rolling along despite all the persistent changes in technologies, markets, and consumer needs. This will allow for a swift adoption of emerging technologies to become a major part of our success.

A shift toward new technologies will result in a shift in organizational structure. Old departments will become stakeholders in new technologies and machines, and old employees will begin focusing on new tasks. Departments will shift and turn, and hierarchies will pivot and change.

Even so, one thing remains true: It is up to each person to rise to the occasion and learn a new skill to stay relevant in the workforce and evolve as organizational structures evolve. Some people will jump on board, others will resist the change. A good leader will approach digital transformation with this in mind and speak to the concerns holding people back in moving forward.

Chapter 14

Change Impact on People

Processes, people, and technology are all connected by change. There is no change within one pillar of an organization that will not impact another, and it's safe to say that any shift in processes or technology will impact the people behind the operation. It's critical to think through the cohesive, downstream impact any adjustments to people, processes, or technology might have. We must dig below the surface. By doing so, we'll have a better understanding of how team dynamics and specific responsibilities within impact roles will be affected.

Say we've recently gone through an assessment of our manufacturing processes for our best-selling product. After going through this exercise, we determined that a small adjustment in the way we meld plastic will drive efficiencies in our operations. It will allow us to meet demand in a more practical manner, making it the most optimal solution to shorten production times and eliminate bottlenecks within the manufacturing line. Joe, a tenured employee responsible for the melding process, will just need to be trained on the new workflow, and we should be good to go, right? This is where a lot of executives trip up.

It is not just one, small change. It's not just one employee who will be impacted. Sure, it's only one piece of a greater manufacturing process, but we must open our eyes to how that pivot will impact others up and downstream.

On the surface, it may appear as though Joe will simply need to learn the new process of melding the plastic. However, it's only when we take a step back that the greater impact becomes apparent. Joe is going to have to change multiple elements of how he does his job. Everything from the materials ordered to how he enters production data in the system will shift. Beyond that, Roger in procurement will need to understand the different quantities or supplies needed to accommodate the change. There may be new parts that need to be ordered or a new material that might cost a bit more than the original. If the new materials cost more, the price we charge the end-user may increase. If that's the case, it would affect Lisa on the web development team to update the website accordingly, and it will require Fransisco in sales to shift his sales approach to accommodate a higher price point. It may even impact Sarah on the fulfillment team if the weight of the product varies from what it was prior to the change, or the production time is much shorter so her team could get the product into shipping quicker than they had before.

It goes beyond one small change. It goes beyond Joe. In fact, it touches multiple levels of the organization, and unless we are aware of that impact, we will likely run into some level of operational disruption. This example illustrates the trickle-down effect of one, seemingly small process change. It's no wonder that many overlook the concept of organizational change management, especially when a change seems insignificant at first. The impact of change is often diluted and difficult to visualize at first glance. How hard could it really be for Joe to apply one additional step in a process he already knows? A change that impacts only Joe at first glance can turn out to be a change that impacts multiple people, teams, and maybe even multiple departments across the workflow.

Joe's example is a relatively easy one to understand as far as change impact goes. However, it becomes much more complex when it comes to pivoting core processes and technologies through a digital transformation. Regardless of the size of the change, the same stands true – managing the human aspect of a transformation can make or break the success of our overarching digital strategy.

There are several critical work streams within change management, such as organizational design and the redefinition of employee roles and responsibilities as we discussed in previous chapters. If we plan to completely automate the plastic melding process and implement robotics to get the job done, it's important to define and communicate the change to Joe and the surrounding touch points of his role *early on*. Prior to making a change, we should first consider the impact that implementation will have and understand how individuals and workgroups within our organization are going to be affected by the transformation. With that, we can craft our communications, training, and change efforts around the needs of the people who will be overseeing and executing the new process.

Without this intentional effort, people will succumb to an apprehensive mindset and think that robots will take over their jobs. They may become hesitant to adopt new processes that support the transformation, causing both intentional and unintentional resistance to change. An intentional approach to communicating and training employees is the foundation of appropriate and effective change management.

Chapter 15

How to Convey the Vision

Up to this point, we've discussed the importance of organizational change management, how it impacts business transformation success and the repercussions of neglecting it through the formulation of a digital strategy. Now that we know how important it is to the launch, we now need to talk about just how to do it. Where do we start when formulating an organizational change management plan? When should the planning begin? What are the key elements that need to be included in the plan? When do we start communicating with employees, and what do we say?

The key to successful organizational change management is to initiate communications and training with the greater team straight out of the gate. As a matter of fact, we can never start the process too early. Far too many organizations wait until the end of a digital transformation to address the change with their greater team, leaving employees with doubts all too close to go live.

Understand that there will be resistance, and there will be hesitation. It's inevitable, and the goal of a change management plan should be to mitigate that resistance and ensure everyone feels as comfortable as possible with the new normal by the time it launches. As soon as we set foot on the journey of piecing together a digital strategy and executing a digital transformation, it's time to outline a change management strategy. It starts at the beginning, and the conceptualization and execution of change management will intertwine with the overall digital strategy from start to finish. Let's unravel the five components of initiating a strong organizational change management strategy that gets organizations from their current state to their future state.

5 steps to jump-starting change management efforts.

Perform an organizational readiness assessment.

Even in a scenario where all our employees are excited to utilize new, up-to-date technology, we will always experience some degree of pushback. Many times, leaders think that everyone across the organization is tired of their system from the early 2000s and can't wait for an upgrade. That may be the case, but even so, resistance rarely manifests itself upfront.

Resistance to change comes once the change approaches and begins to impact someone's day-to-day. The purpose of performing an organizational readiness assessment is to uncover the level at which people will resist change, what the root causes of resistance are, and what pockets of the organization will push back on the changes coming down the pipeline. In this phase, we will be able to shine a light on obstacles such as perceived misalignment, communication breakdowns from department to department, and even a negative perception of top-down management – all components that can hinder the success of a digital transformation.

Perform a change impact assessment.

This assessment differs from an organizational readiness assessment in the sense that it looks more closely at the tangible changes that will hit the existing organizational structure. It digs deeper into the departments, teams, and individual roles and responsibilities that will evolve as a result of the transformation. This step is imperative to the overarching digital strategy as it plays into mapping out the new processes that come with a transformation, and ultimately the software that will best help our organizations fulfill those new processes.

By understanding how jobs will be impacted and what new roles will look like with new technology, a natural sense of alignment and buy-in is born. When people are in the loop, they feel like they are a part of the change. When there is inconsistency or a lack of transparency, the opposite is true and resistance takes the lead. Those who will be impacted by a given change need to understand how their roles will be redefined, how teams will work together, and how their relevant organizational structure will shift. This information will help craft communication and training plans to better prepare people for the changes to come.

Assess and ensure internal alignment.

Alignment on the trajectory of the company needs to be crystal clear. From executives down to mid-level management, everyone needs to be moving at the same stroke toward the same future state. If the mission and journey are clearly outlined, all sails will point in the same direction. Are we looking to make quantum leap changes in our operations, or are we simply trying to improve efficiencies? Are we trying to increase revenue by cutting costs or driving more sales? Our organizational assessment in step one will help identify these slight nuances, but it's integral that a third party is introduced to address any potential misalignment. Hire an independent consultant that can assess the team's greater perceptions and identify any silos in alignment. If they identify silos, it's best that a third party addresses them to help get everyone on the same page without ruffled feathers.

Assemble your change team

There should be a team of people that spearhead all change management efforts – the change team. This should be an internal group of employees that leads all communication, training, and strategic change management efforts. Yes, external resources can also be used here, but be careful. A system integrator will sell themselves on the fact that they can also assist with change management. Don't fall for it. A system integrator's focus is on how to enable new technologies, they are not focused on change and the internal team. Again, that's like a plumber coming in to tell us that they can also do dry-walling. It just doesn't work that way. The best external resource available to support the change team would be a technology-agnostic consultant. This is especially true if no one on the internal change team has experience with change management.

Another thing to note is that stakeholders should be spread out across different focuses of the digital transformation. Although we have a change team that's particularly responsible for change management, the best approach to a successful operational change management strategy is to share the weight. The change team will spearhead the majority of the work, but everyone on the project team should have some type of change management responsibility.

Consider looking further beyond a designated project and change team, and bring on influencers within the organization to help the cause. Train the influencers before the general team, and they will act as a dedicated resource for their more granular teams and peers. With this approach, everyone on the project team will have skin in the game and know who to go to with any questions, improving the odds of implementing a more successful operational change management strategy.

Create your change strategy.

This is it. Once we've checked off the first four steps, it's time to actually use the information we've acquired and the teams we've created to craft our overall change management strategy. As we map out this plan, we must keep in mind that there is no such thing as an out-of-the-box, cookie-cutter change management strategy. There is no silver bullet in alleviating change struggles for a company or a team. Each strategy needs to be tailored to the unique characteristics of the company, such as its culture, its projected resistance, its alignment status, and its overall attitude toward change.

Change management consists primarily of two components – communication and training. With that said, each of these components consists of multiple tactics that must be adhered to to drive an effective change strategy. Let's, break down how we formulate change strategy and plan our communication and training initiatives.

Communication Planning

Dialing in on an effective communication plan requires us to dig below the surface. Of course, we have to communicate the progress of a project, maybe even timelines and goals. However, we need to do this in a very intentional way. When discussing a communication plan, we must think of why we will communicate, how we will communicate, and what we will communicate.

Why are we communicating?

This question will be answered the same every time. All communications that go out to the organization need to be spoken through the lens of *what's in it for me*. The person on the other end of the communication needs to understand how this will impact them specifically. It's important to make sure we're not only focusing on project-specific information. Communicate milestones and what's next in the project through a targeted approach for each group in the organization. Think of how different teams and departments will be impacted, as that will likely shift communications from group to group. Be intentional and tailor communications to address any resistance that may have been identified during the organizational assessment.

Again, it's important to share how the new process and technology will enable the company to reach its goals, but that is never going to be the main message. The main message must revolve around how the individual's role will become easier in some way or another. Think about how the new way of operating will bring less stress to their day-to-day life by alleviating pain points they may have dealt with in the past. When we approach communications from this angle, resistance will dwindle and buy-in will increase.

How will we communicate?

Some people check their email consistently. Some may communicate more effectively via phone or video calls. Others may take more kindly to live, in-person interactions, or maybe on-demand content that they can refer to when they have time. Create a diverse communication plan that lays out messages through various communication channels. When creating a communication plan, incorporate email as a baseline, and sprinkle in seminars. Put up flyers around the office that outline the benefits of the change, almost like an advertisement for the new normal to come. Schedule ongoing webinars and conference calls, and encourage mid-level management to facilitate meetings. An organizational assessment should identify the preferred means of communication by the greater team, so utilize that information when determining where to focus communication efforts. No matter the communication medium, the goal should be to deliver a fairly uniform message crafted around the *'why'*.

What?

While crafting a communication plan, it doesn't hurt to draft what each communication looks like across the different phases of the project. Create a timeline of communications that will be followed as the project progresses. As long as we stay flexible in our communications and add or adjust messaging as the nature of the project changes, we will benefit from planning the specific messaging in advance.

The anatomy of a communication plan should always enable a two-way conversation. In addition to sharing information on the new technology, it's critical to get information from the recipients of the change as well. Gauge how people are responding by keeping a supervised forum for people to discuss concerns and ideas anonymously. Enable question-and-answer sessions to answer open-ended questions as the change approaches. When a two-way conversation is enabled, people feel more a part of the shift rather than a byproduct of the shift.

Listening is critical to the success of a digital transformation. The perspective of a project team is often completely wrong when they are assessing the strengths and weaknesses of the front lines. Those sitting in an ivory tower do not know the intricacies of a given warehouse role. They do not fully grasp the bottlenecks and friction points of a manufacturing line. If we are sitting in a conference room laying out what a business process should entail, but the people who really know how processes work (those on the floor) are not in the room, there will be holes in the outlined process. Rather than asking what they think of a process change, get into the weeds with them. Layout the new proposed process and ask them how it compares to the old process. Ask them how they think their job will be impacted by the given process change. The goal is to understand the full scope of their feedback, and that can be done by creating formal and informal feedback centers for frontline workers to share their perspectives.

On the other end of the two-way communication plan, it's critical to understand our audience. A lot of organizations have people working on shop floors or in the warehouse, so it requires a bit of creativity in how to get a hold of them. These workers are not checking emails, and they're unlikely to get on a conference call. Sometimes, we have to climb out of our ivory tower and find a different way to communicate. At the end of the day, these people are the ones who have the most power in the success or failure of a new process or technology implementation.

Communicating anticipated changes in roles and responsibilities could be something that ignites fear and resistance in those very people who hold the power to make things work. It can be a scary conversation for people on both ends of the communication. So, how do we broach it? First, it's important to fully recognize and appreciate how things are in their current state. Many people jump ahead to talking about the company's future state – the mission and vision for the future and the goals and objectives that sparked the change. However, the business, as it is today, was built around the existing processes and culture. Once we understand and embrace the current state of business in our messaging and general digital transformation, we can paint a better picture of where the company plans to go in five to ten years.

Now that we know the foundational elements to a communication plan, let's look at an example of a large gas and electric firm. This industry has always dealt with constantly shifting regulations as the political climate changed over time. These shifts in the industry environment led to a need for change that would push the company to a more modernized state. On one hand, they had a vision for the future of where they wanted to be, but on the other hand, they had a very tenured team of employees who had been there for years and were hesitant to change.

If this was our company's landscape for a digital transformation, we would need to create a detailed plan with people in the organization that would outline all communication efforts. We would involve different stakeholders, from executives to frontline employees, to help dial in on the entire transformation. Once we mapped out our general digital transformation plan, we would begin our communication efforts. We can follow this step-by-step approach when developing a communication plan.

Step 1

Map out a timeline of the project and pair it with a timeline of communications. Plan out the general timeframe in which you will send out announcements, key milestones, status updates, seminars and training schedules, and any other information that is helpful to the transformation project.

Step 2

Write, create and schedule the distribution of videos, emails, seminars, training, and even flyers to be posted around the building so they are ready to go come distribution time. Ensure flyers can be updated as needed as you progress through the project.

Step 3

Craft the core of the message around *what's in it for me*, but try to customize every message, especially at the forefront of the project, for each department. The reason? Each department will likely have varying motivations. Sales will be money motivated whereas accounting might be efficiency motivated. Express how the change will make a department's efforts more efficient. Talk about how roles and responsibilities will become less occupied with busy work, allowing for more time to create and produce results?

Step 4

Create an open communication forum and round tables where people can ask questions and play a role in the development of the change. Consider a team forum where the employees can make the choice of if they want to communicate as themselves or remain anonymous. That ambiguity and empowerment will help drive conversation.

Step 5

Continue to communicate long after going live to check in with the team members and make sure everyone has acclimated to the new way of working.

Another key element to crafting a sound communication plan is to be aware of the red flags that point to faulty communications. When objectively looking at a communication plan, it's important to keep an eye out for certain warning signs. This is such a pivotal component of our overarching strategy that if there is even a whiff of subpar communication efforts from the project and/or change team, then it needs to be addressed immediately. The red flags to look for may include the following:

- A project team does not fully understand the level of awareness across the rest of the organization.
- Focusing solely on project updates.
- Project communication teams that focus too much on project updates only.
- Communications around solely how the company will benefit and grow from the new changes.

Training

Training is the easy part of an organizational change management plan. The biggest piece is making sure that the training is not held at the very last minute before going live with the new processes and technologies. This is a pitfall that many organizations trip on, and it sabotages all efforts to mitigate resistance. The goal is to pair training and communications like a fine wine and an aged cheese. The two should be planned and operating in harmony so that communications T-up successful training.

If communications are planned and distributed appropriately, then the natural resistance will happen long before any training begins. This should always be the goal. The last thing anyone wants is to have heavy realizations about the shift in their job role in the middle of a training. Rather, those freakouts need to happen and be addressed months before through strategic and targeted communications.

We want people to walk into training knowing how their role will change so the training can focus on how to execute upon their new role and facilitate new processes. In addition to training earlier, consider training in segments.

An influencer on a smaller team is typically an individual contributor who has a great reputation among their peers. They seem to get along well with others and have the trust of their fellow coworkers. Have managers identify these people and make them their team's designated subject matter experts. Bring these subject matter experts into the training earlier than others to ensure that they can understand the new processes and technologies well enough to act as a resource for their immediate team and peers.

By incorporating influencers in our training strategy, we will further help mitigate resistance.

It's easy to get caught up in the training portion of a change plan, but understand that this is truly the easiest part. Don't get too caught up on this portion. Simply schedule the training and move along. Focus more on the processes and the people before focusing on how to operate new technology. Let the *strategy* lead the technology, the training, and the communications.

At the end of the day, 95% of people want to change. Employees only start to resist when they don't fully understand what a change means for them. By integrating these tactics into our organizational change management strategy, we will open the door for great technologies and new processes that could launch our operations into orbit.

Chapter 16

Next Steps: Developing an Organizational Change Plan

Let's take a reflective look at our organization, specifically. This chapter will provide the framework needed to perform an organizational assessment of the *People* side of our business that will funnel into our overarching digital strategy. This assessment should capture information about peoples' communication preferences, their motivations, their current trust in leadership, and their appetite for change.

It's more than email communications. It's more than trainings held once a week. It's more than just sharing information. We need to peel back the layers of each chapter as it relates to our business and formulate a strategy. To get started on your own organizational change management strategy, follow these steps:

Step 1

Facilitate a survey to assess the organization's appetite for change.

Create and facilitate an online survey to uncover some of the root causes of resistance that may occur. The survey should:

- Allow surveyors to answer questions anonymously.
- Take about 10-15 minutes to complete.
- Be structured to uncover possible resistance in a quantitative way (this is the overarching goal of the assessment). For example, ask pointed questions to gauge trust in leadership, motivations for performance, and belief levels in company mission statements.

Step 2

Define qualitative and quantitative data that points to resistance.

Create focus groups to define the qualitative reasons behind the quantitative data of resistance found in the survey. Who is resistant to change?

Why are they resistant? What are the attributes of their current comfort zones? What do they like about their job, and what are they proud of?

Step 3

Craft communications.

Take this information and map out a content-based communication strategy. What are we going to say to people, and when? Outline the message first, then schedule it.

Step 4

Evolve communications into various mediums.

Once we have the message or messages, create a communication timeline that includes the various channels of communication we will use to deliver our different messages. Repurpose the same message into different delivery methods such as:

- Video Conferences
- Live Meetings
- Phone Conferences
- Video
- Email
- Events
- Flyers

Step 5

Map out training efforts.

Plan out a training timeline and define strategies our team will use to facilitate those trainings. Keep the following in mind:

- Once we select a software and begin getting acquainted, select influencers and subject matter experts to include in the first wave of trainings.

- Once the influencers and subject matter experts are trained, enable them to lead their peers in adopting the new processes and technologies.
  - General trainings begin thereafter, and should be held in various formats such as seminars, live coaching sessions, videos, or text.

Step 6

Define a change management sustainability plan.

Just because it seems everyone is excited to implement new technology and everything seems to be going well, it doesn't mean our change management efforts can stop. Continuously check in with mid-level managers and the greater team to gauge the success rate of the adoption of the new processes and technology. Consider the following:

- Is there anyone struggling?
- Is anyone using their old spreadsheet on the side, or reverting back to old processes?
- Take satisfaction surveys.

From here, create a plan for those who may not be fully onboard and reward those who have fully embraced the new changes.

Throughout the journey in building a future state, never forget that the people factor is the most important element to seeing success in any digital and corporate strategy. The support we provide to our employees on their journey is pivotal to the success of our overarching transformation. If there is any section to come back to or do more research on, let it be the art of managing change in people.

PART III
Technology

Chapter 17

The Launching Pad

From the inception of server-based enterprise resource planning to the countless cloud solutions available on the market, the journey of advancing technology has been one that has forever changed the way companies operate. It's incredible looking at where the world of enterprise technology began and what it has become. Today's world of best-of-breed options and full-scope ERP solutions stand on the shoulders of the founding fathers of enterprise technology, and it's evolved rather quickly within the past few decades.

It was in the 1960s when the concept of utilizing a system to manage processes came to fruition. As a joint effort between a large construction machinery manufacturer and IBM, the venture to create software that would help in the manufacturing process commenced. This project led to the creation of a software known as Materials Requirements Planning, or an MRP software.

As time went on, MRP systems helped plan raw material requirements for manufacturing, purchasing, and delivery. The system caught wind in the 1970s and led to new developments in the years to come. It was in 1972 that the firm, SAP, launched in Germany. SAP, short for Systemanalyse Programmentwicklung, which translates to System Analysis Program Development, was an absolute breakthrough in a world of punch cards. They developed the world's first, real-time computing software that could collect and process data. A year later, in 1973, SAP launched its first financial accounting system that opened the door for more focused software developments to hit the market.[3]

In 1977, both JD Edwards and Oracle were born. One by one, the big players entered the market, offering business solutions to organizations locally. As the companies grew, they began to provide services to both domestic and international organizations. It began with on-premise solutions that ran off of

---

3 "What is SAP?", SAP.com website, accessed August 2022, https://www.sap.com/about/company/what-is-sap.html

company servers. This novel approach at the time improved efficiency and data management enabling companies to grow further within each industry that leveraged them. With more tech-induced opportunities, society as a whole slowly advanced further and further as a result.

Of course, systems such as SAP and Oracle had hefty server requirements, meaning that only the big-hitters and larger organizations had access to utilizing enterprise software at that point. It wasn't until the 1990s when the term 'ERP' first came to light and automating more focused business functions such as engineering, finance, accounting, HR, and project management began. It was barely just a decade later that Netsuite paved the way for cloud based ERP systems. Netsuite became the first company to provide business application solutions over the internet, and they started a wave that has become today's norm: Cloud Computing.

It was in the early 2000s that the consolidations began. The big players began acquiring the little players. Mergers and acquisitions within the industry are still going strong today. Fast forward to the 21st century and all enterprise software is migrating to the cloud, delivering both full scope ERP solutions and focused, best of breed solutions.

The market has become diversified and nearly overwhelming. With new and emerging technologies flooding the innovations of this technology-driven era, it can be hard to keep up with which software is the right fit for our organization. Should we harness the power of AI and robotics into our operations, or are we in a position that would most benefit from a simple upgrade in our inventory management system?

By understanding the current landscape of the technology market and comparing it with where our company's existing technology landscape sits, we can better gauge how much room there is to grow. It starts with getting a clear clutch on the current capabilities, skills, and functionalities of our existing systems. If we have the bare minimum systems in place, it will be a much bigger leap to implement emerging technologies. That's not to say it's not doable, but the change impact will be much greater and it will require a more thorough assessment of all aspects of our organization's people, processes and technologies.

Dive into the gap. How big is the gap between where we are today and where we want to go in regards to the available technologies on the market? The reality of digital transformation is that we can't fully grasp the potential we hold until we know where we currently stand. Before we jump into the technical elements of a digital strategy, such as software selections and implementation planning, let's first start with the current technology landscape our organization lives in.

When it comes to digital transformation, the main points to consider are *who* and *what* will be up for a change. Typically, a project will be initiated to solve a problem or to introduce a new function within the business. The usual approach is to understand and capture the business and systems requirements and align them to the business objectives outlined in the business case. Sounds easy, but it isn't always so simple. We have to be crystal clear on which technologies, which processes, and which people will be affected by the digital transformation initiative. Often times companies want to throw out the current state, and dive directly into the future state (if you've been paying attention up to this point, you know that that is not going to work). We will get to the future state at some point, but in order to get there, we have to know where we are starting.

In order to get a solid grip on where we are today, we must perform (you guessed it) an assessment focused on the IT sector of our organization. To do this, we must dial down on three factors that serve as the foundation to our organization's technological capabilities.

1. Systems and Applications
2. System Architecture
3. Data Management

At the end of Part III, I will walk you through the steps of performing your own organizational assessment, but here are some high-level thoughts to let marinade until we get there.

Systems and Applications

In this part of the assessment, we will dissect the current systems in place keeping in mind the context of our general IT infrastructure. We must guage the various aspects of our current digital model that are working. What processes are currently being optimized that we would like to hold on to or mirror in our future state operating model?

Even in the scenario that we are overhauling our entire enterprise resource planning software for a new, cleaner system, there are likely still components of the existing model that work fairly well with current operations. The question becomes, will those processes stick around as we evolve to the future state? If the answer is yes, write those processes and IT functionalities down, and prioritize them to stand as a deciding factor throughout software evaluations.

On the other side of the coin, there are likely bottlenecks and hurdles in the current technology that we're excited to replace with something more effective and efficient. We should take inventory of those needs as well. This will help us build and improve on some of the best practices in the marketplace that we have yet to capitalize on.

System Architecture

When we consider our existing tech landscape beyond the individual systems, we see a big web of computers and software that communicate with each other. We should evaluate those webs and become very familiar with our existing integrations. By understanding how each system is connected to the next, we'll be able to identify synergies and silos that exist across our current IT landscape.

Just like we took inventory with our independent applications and systems, we must take inventory of the way the applications and systems communicate with each other. There will be good things that we'll want to take with us, such as an unquestionable connection between two systems that work closely together. For example, does our CRM connect with our accounting software, and if so, what does that process look like? Maybe it's the way that a closed sale translates into revenue listed on the balance sheet. Maybe it's a process that tracks sales rep's commissions and funnels them into payroll. Whatever that process may be, we must identify it as it relates to our existing systems so that we can easily transfer that process into a new system.

In this day and age, functionality is a must have for a business and that functionality should stay intact as we venture toward our future state. In another instance, we may find that our CRM is not allowing for specifications to be included in a new order that is then passed to manufacturing. Maybe sales representatives have to update manufacturing with the specifications of a new project each time a new client is closed. This is not sustainable, and it's a big opportunity to streamline workflows as our organization dials in on a new software solution. In this scenario, the technology we are looking for would have the expanded functionality to customize each sale before it goes to accounting. This way, accounting gets the full scope of accurate data points while manufacturing gets the full scope order details and customizations straight out of the gate. Hello, scalability.

In general, system design is an important step to execute before jumping straight into ERP implementation. Our goal is to map this out just as we mapped out our processes, and we should understand the integration points that exist in our current system architecture. Once we have that understanding in our back pocket, it's time to jump into the integrations and connections we'd like our system to have in the future state. What components of our organization should speak to each other through the utilization of technology? Going through this exercise will allow us to think about how the components of our business relate to one another in the grand scheme of things. Due to the fact that an ERP system connects to accounting, warehouse management, logistics, etc., laying out a system that allows us to quickly understand the relationship between these components can be incredibly valuable.

Data Management

To take it one step further, we need to analyze how data flows through these integration points from system to system. Siloed operations are the biggest villain here because they can result in multiple data sets. Through this assessment, we'll be able to get a clear grasp on where the data currently resides. We'll be able to dial in on the one source with the most accurate data so that the data migration efforts will be more seamless and efficient.

Many times, organizations need to do ample pre-work as it relates to cleansing and scrubbing data to ensure only accurate data enters the new system. By addressing this component at the forefront of a digital transformation, we're able to knock out two birds with one stone: assessing our current digital landscape while also preparing to migrate to a new landscape.

Once we have a clear vision of our business strategy and we dial in on where we want our organization to go, we begin doubling down on the enterprise applications that can help us get there. This is where it can be helpful to look to the market to see what new modern technologies could help us take that quantum leap to get to where our business wants to go.

There is always an opportunity to improve, but the reality is there are always different risk profiles. By looking at the current state of these three sections of our IT landscape, we are able to determine the next step. We'll get a glimpse into whether or not it makes the most sense to jump in and make one big change all at once, or if we should solely focus on improving our processes and stop there.

It comes down to identifying the roadmap that makes the most sense for our organization. No organization should ever jump on new technology because they think it'll solve all their problems. We must implement technology that we know will streamline and address efficiencies that are needed in order to intentionally grow and scale.

Let's take Joe as an example. Joe has been tasked with replacing his current minivan with a new vehicle to help get him and his family from point A to point B. He has a big budget, so he runs out and buys a red Ferrari. Why? Because it not only satisfies the requirement of going from point A to point B, but it'll get him to point B faster. It also has all the bells and whistles, and he will look super cool. Bob at the dealership said it would make him look like he'll mean business.

What Joe overlooked was a handful of other factors outside of said requirements. His wife and kids that would also need to ride in the car, the various car seats he would have to fit in the backseat, the fact that his local mechanic has no idea how to do an oil change on a Ferrari, the daily and weekly errands he would have to run in this car to keep life moving at the right pace – the list goes on.

If Joe did an assessment of his current state to become more clear on what was and wasn't working and ultimately understand the true needs he'd have to meet, he would have made a better decision on which car to get. He may have even found that he really just needed new tires and an oil change on the minivan in order for it to meet the need. The bottom line is, Joe didn't do his due diligence to make the Ferrari a viable, functional option.

When we begin looking at digital transformation projects, it's easy to get distracted by all the shiny functionalities that come with the innovative systems on the market. A higher budget comes with shinier options and a riskier investment. Shiny-object syndrome almost always leads to blurred vision when the vision isn't rooted in purpose and strategy. Stay focused. Don't get distracted by the bells and whistles and overlook the assessment phase of our current landscape, its needs, and its limits.

Chapter 18

Visualizing The Future

When I was a kid, I thought that 2020 was the year we would have flying cars and robots making us breakfast. The visionaries behind the global tech had different plans. Although our cars still have wheels, it's no question about just how far technology has come within the past 20 years. As we look at the trajectories of where technology is headed, we must first be considerate of our organizations' future state. By discussing both in the same breath, we enable ourselves to find the best-fit technology that we can leverage over the next several years without falling behind as new innovations hit the market.

The technologies we invest in today will likely be with us over the next five to ten years. During that time, technology will evolve tenfold. In order to stay competitive, we want to select processes and technologies now that will keep our organization relevant and differentiated even as others adopt new technologies over the next several years.

In addition to that awareness of constantly evolving technology comes the vision we paint for ourselves that will guide us into the future. Yes, maybe technology will unlock the possibility of robot chefs making breakfast in the morning over the next five years, but what will our company be doing? Where will it be in the next five, ten, fifteen years? What will we be known for? The bridge to getting there stands on the three pillars of digital transformation: Processes, people, and technology.

We discussed the concept of our future state in Chapter 3, but I want to touch on it once more as it relates to the future state of our in-house technology. In the tech-driven world we live in today, our enterprise technology (paired with strong strategies behind our people and processes) has the potential to differentiate our level of service and our brand. It's the efficiencies that come with finding the best fit software that can unlock doors to a new or refined competitive edge.

In order to attain that, we must first know what we want that competitive edge to look like. A company's future state translates to a greater vision for the business. For a company to truly reach its potential, it must understand and harness its superpowers, envisioning what it would look like if those superpowers reached their full potential. By dialing in on the elements of our business that set us apart, we can more effectively prioritize the capabilities of the future software that could streamline our journey to our future state.

So, what are those elements that set our organization apart from the competition? Do we have stellar customer service? What about our customer service makes us so great? Maybe we have the highest quality product on the market in our industry. If so, what part of the production process leads to that level of quality?

The first step to the entire digital transformation process is painting that vivid illustration for our organization's leadership team that explains what our business will be known in five to ten years. It's our corporate strategy, it's point A, the starting point, in all that we do through our technology initiatives. From there, it takes drilling down to the processes that make our company unique and prioritizing those processes as we explore software options.

When focusing on the technology pillar of our digital transformation, our attention should be on the technologies that could best accommodate our prioritized processes – the processes that set our organization apart from the rest. In the current digital climate, many companies think that in order to stay ahead in their industry, they need to stay ahead in the technological functionalities of their organization as well. While there is a level of truth to this, this isn't always the case. Going from A to C is a much more manageable journey than going from A to Z. It's doable, it will just require a greater deal of preparation before the actual implementation begins.

Too often, organizations jump into adopting robotics, artificial intelligence, and other modern technologies for their operations when they simply aren't ready. Just because these technologies are proving to drive efficiencies and scalability doesn't mean it's the right technology for our unique operations.

Although emerging technologies such as AI and RPA are at the forefront of scaling businesses into high-volume growth, not all organizations are ready to take the plunge. Many technology innovation journeys fail to meet expectations when it comes to time and budget. Rarely is failure a result of technical issues, but rather organizational issues. Problems with integrating people with the technology, appropriate data management strategies, and having clear business processes can all lead to major delays and cost overruns. Without proper preparation and planning, even the most sophisticated technology can quickly become a costly white elephant. This is especially true when it comes to implementing emerging technologies.

Is our business ready to embrace the new wave of emerging technologies? We should rightsize our organization before we even consider implementing emerging and modern technologies as a part of our digital strategy. Here are a handful of hindrances that could be holding our company back from adopting modern technologies into our operations.

Poor Data Management

When we notice things like dirty data, a lack of consensus around where the data is stored, or find repeated or unmatched data, we know there are issues with the data structure and how the company is utilizing and strategizing data management tactics. The problem is, it happens more often than we think, and the mountains of big data can easily fly off the rails if there isn't intention put behind it.

A lack of clean data can lead to things like unanswered insights or even a misunderstanding of business processes. For example, if we're going to implement new software that's built on automation, we should make sure the data is *actionable* in order to create business value. Without the storytelling aspect of data, it's just a bunch of units of information. We also need to understand where the data is housed and be able to make sense of it.

Ask questions like:

- Is there a data warehouse?

- Are there other systems in which there might be unmined data, like a financial system, an additional application, or a CRM system that is not integrated with our data management structure?
- What are the reporting capabilities around that data?
- How is the data consumed?
- How can we create actionable strategies from the data we have now?

Any strong operational strategy must have a master data management plan. It's important to have a centralized and organized process around data management before we look at technologies that utilize it to enhance our processes. This is the foundational to technology. By doing ensuring our data is ready for migration, we can ensure that our business is ready to leap from technology on the market ten years ago to technology on the market today.

Business Processes

It's essential to have clear visibility – from end-to-end – of business processes. There must be consistency in mapping those processes to identify opportunities or understand flaws that will hinder the impact that emerging tech can have on operations.

If we don't have a clear understanding of business processes within our organization, then implementing an emerging technology can be completely irrelevant.

The technology won't be able to function correctly, and it will create technical debt from a lack of business value for our investment.

Business Culture

It's important to evaluate our business culture and understand the infrastructure of our organization. There are certain factors related to our company culture that will help us measure our team's appetite for emerging technologies.

Ask questions like:

- Do you have siloed departments or are there processes that other departments might not understand?
- Is there a culture of cross-collaboration within your organization?
- Will your organization's culture allow you to take data from one department and integrate it into another? Will it allow you to utilize something like AI or predictive analytics to create strategies?
- Do your people have a misperception of what AI is? Do they have a "robots take over" approach in creating fear around their job function?
- Are there any other misperceptions within your organization around what the technology is used for?

Each element listed above can create fear and disruption among our employees when implementing any new technology, better yet advanced technology, such as AI and robotics, that has been demonized through pop culture films and media. Understanding those areas of resistance will help us craft a strong and strategic organizational change management strategy that is customized to our specific team.

Communication

If we have trouble communicating as an organization, then we should evaluate why there is a breakage. If there is a lack of trust between leadership and employees, then we should evaluate the current rhetoric that could be causing the lack of trust. We should formulate communications that can patch the hole before embarking on a digital transformation journey.

Whether it's a specific employee engagement platform that manages mass communications or sending direct emails to each department and team, communications need to be evaluated and prioritized. If we don't have a productive communication strategy in place, implementing new technology could turn out to be dangerous. Ultimately, the investment could fall flat without proper communication strategies that hold up our overarching organizational change management strategy. Without a proper plan in place, there will be an inability to centralize the communications around the project.

A lack of transparency alone has the power to kill our investment in a digital transformation. If people on our team are not aware of the plan to integrate emerging technology in some capacity, we risk a lack of user adoption come go live. This is especially true if our team is naturally hesitant toward emerging technologies and doesn't welcome the idea of robots making breakfast in the morning.

Organizational Change Management

Having a clear organizational change management, or OCM, plan is critical to being able to communicate and identify areas in which the new technology might affect someone's experience in the organization, their roles, or their responsibilities. OCM, or a lack thereof, is the number one failure point for a rather simple reason: Businesses get ahead of themselves and implement this new technology, but they forget the human factor that's ultimately critical to successful implementation and user adoption.

It's easy to overlook the human element of any emerging technology simply because these new technologies are so good at doing the tactical elements of our current jobs. But, if we fall blind to the empathy that makes up our human DNA, the one piece that no robot or computer can embody on a genuine level, then we are destined to lose in the long run. Whether it be the support of our employee base or the buy-in from our consumers. People want to interact with people to one extent or another. Losing sight of that will actually put us at a disadvantage when it comes to crafting a strong competitive advantage.

IT Capabilities

Our IT capabilities and systems architecture should also be a consideration when determining whether or not emerging technology is the right fit. If our IT team is not familiar with managing robotics, we either need to hire new talent or invest in equipping the team to rise to the occasion. Again, it's doable, but it will likely take more time, money, and resources to get to the finish line. The bridge from A to B only needs a handful of bricks and labor, the bridge from A to Z needs much more.

As discussed in the previous chapter, our first step before jumping into any technology, emerging or not, is to perform an organizational assessment. We should evaluate where we are today and what our current resources can handle. If it's out of the ballpark, we need a thorough plan in place to help bridge the gap between where we are today and where we want to be. The greater the leap, the more resources it'll take to arrive at the destination.

Today's business landscape forces us to tie together our vision for our business and the ample capabilities that modern technology can bring to the table. The two go hand in hand. In today's tech-driven society, one cannot function without the other. Dialing in on our future state will always be our first step. From there, we will pair the best fit technology to speak to the objective set forth to get from point A to point B… or Z.

It feels like a constant race between technology companies to create and innovate, and that's why the industry is evolving ever so quickly. Who knows? The computer was originally created for business uses, and it was years later that it trickled into the consumer market. The same could be true for artificial intelligence and robotics. Emerging technologies are a part of the software selection on the enterprise level today, but one day soon, we could be eating pancakes made by our very own robot.

Chapter 19

The Guard Rails

Let's go back to the parallels between building a home and spearheading a digital transformation. We can all agree that the architect who picks up the shovel before drawing a blueprint will build a subpar home. The home is bound to have some level of structural issues down the line, and the floor plan may not be as well thought out as it could have been. It was rushed. In fact, the average architect takes about four months in the planning phase before they submit construction documents and permit applications to build.[4] Some may take even longer.

It's a process, and there is no way to cut corners without compromising the quality of the job. The same is true for a business that implements new software without a roadmap. Without a cohesive and detailed plan of action, there are bound to be holes in the end result. That plan of action should be outlined, in detail, in the business case.

Many leaders pour too little into their business case, approaching it as if it's just a means of getting approval on a digital transformation project. It's more than a tool for approvals. Much more. The reality is that in order to reach success in our digital transformation, a business case must be more than just a pitch deck. When done correctly, it becomes the bible of our digital transformation project, with scriptures that will guide us through the good times and the bad. Beyond that, it can evolve into our greater implementation plan

When it comes time to make decisions on if we should bolt on a new application that streamlines specific parts of our operations more than initially scoped, we will refer to our business case. When it comes time to make decisions around changing or adjusting a business process to fit technology, we will refer to our business case. A business case acts as our guide, with goals

---

4 "How Long Does It Take for an Architect to Draw Up Plans?" Denny + Gardner Remodeling Building Design Website, November 20, 2021, https://www.dennyandgardner.com/blog/how-long-architect-plans

and objectives framing the decisions we make along the way. If the decision meets the greater objectives of the digital transformation, then we should do it. If not, then we shouldn't. It's a way to simplify complex decisions for a robust project and provide a crutch as we begin investing.

Building (yes building, not writing) a business case is the perfect opportunity to design an intricate blueprint and build a plan that not only acts as a means of acquiring vertical and lateral alignment on the digital strategy but also as the guard rails to achieving greater project objectives. It becomes our reference point when big decisions need to be made. It keeps the entire project team and executive team in alignment with the end goal of the transformation. Without it, 'shiny-object syndrome' rooted in each person's own opinion will begin to take charge, and it will put our entire investment at risk.

Whatever the reason may be, many people overlook writing up a business case for an upcoming project. More often than not, a business case is created, but it only scratched the surface of what it can truly be. The reason could range from simply overlooking the value to the need for new technology being so strong that justification is not necessary. Regardless of the reason why people don't do it, it's important to recognize the value a business case can add to a project's overall success rate.

When it comes to our digital transformation, it's no secret that measuring cost vs. benefit when moving to a new ERP platform is critical to the success of the investment. Will there be an improvement in operations that will drive revenue in a way that will make the investment worth it? These systems are expensive and difficult to implement. It will likely detract from other focuses, and we must go into a project like this with that sense of awareness. On the other side of the coin, the cost of doing nothing can be even greater than the cost of implementing a new ERP system.

A solid business case can give leadership confidence that making the move is a good business decision. It will outline the projected costs while also showing the precise, expected outcome at the end. That outcome needs to be intricately drawn as it will represent the future state of our operations. It's this illustration that will guide our decision-making throughout the digital transformation project. Whatever falls on our lap, we will use this illustration as the North Star and move in a way that gets our organization closer to that future state.

Furthermore, a business case should outline the specific metrics that will be measured along the way to ensure the success of the project. To be candid, a majority of digital transformations fail to deliver on time, on budget, and on projected business value. To avoid this, we need to gauge and measure milestone metrics as much as possible throughout the project.

Oftentimes, when transformations fail or neglect to deliver the expected results, it's a surprise to the organization – specifically, the project team and the executives. In some extreme cases, the negative impact on operations wasn't expected or planned for. The key to avoiding this outcome is to understand why disruptions happen, how to mitigate their potential impacts, and deploy KPIs throughout the journey, as well as post-project, to make sure everything stays on track.

At the end of the day, the overarching goal is to ensure that the implementation is on time and within budget. Beyond that, however, comes a need to minimize operational disruption and maximize potential business value. There are several KPIs, or key performance indicators, that can be used to manage and monitor any digital transformation. With those overarching objectives in mind, let's break down a handful of metrics we should always keep at the forefront of our digital transformation projects.

Implementation Time and Cost

The first, and probably most obvious, is overall implementation cost and timing. There are some key questions that may need to be answered before beginning implementations like,

- Are we hitting the milestones of the company?
- Are we going to go live with new technologies on time?

The key to mitigating any risk of overruns on budget and time is to install strong governance and track the process. This governance will live in the business case. It is important to establish limits on time and budget by truly mapping the entire project, from start to finish, and from OCM to data migration. A lot of organizations don't consider the magnitude of different workstreams and budgetary line items within the project plan and strategy. When it's not included in the business case, there is no focal point for the organization to work toward.

Any organization should be able to identify when a project is drifting off track well before it's finished. To identify any drift early on, we must first establish a sound, targeted timeline and a reasonable targeted budget. Know that if we fall behind in the timeline, we will likely incur more fees and charges throughout the project. This will inevitably push us out of budget. The two go hand in hand.

If the company is 25% through the project but has spent 50% of the budget, chances are high that the overall budget will need to be increased. Strong governance and controls along with regular project status reporting will raise the red flag on any potential issues sooner than later. This seems like project management 101, but there's also an art to understanding digital transformations and anticipating risks regarding time and cost.

Operational Readiness

Another key KPI is the overall operational readiness of the organization. Operational readiness is an important part of understanding how well the business processes and technologies are aligned before we go live. Assuming the business processes and requirements in the future state are defined, there should be a measurement system to quantify success and identify any breakdowns in business operations. Consider user acceptance testing and conference room pilots. It is important to think beyond how the technology functions and address full business processes through the different scenarios.

The business plan should outline the intention to test processes and scenarios that will come up as a result of the changes ahead. Of course, before we select the system, we don't have a definite grasp on how things will change, but we will be aware of which processes will be touched and molded. It will be those processes that need to undergo end-to-end testing. This will come through business simulations to test every avenue of operations that have been impacted by the changes in process or technology. As long as we walk into it with full awareness and the expectation that certain things may work while others won't, we will be more nimble and ready to pivot as needed to reach orbit.

Organizational Readiness

Like operational readiness, it is also important to measure organizational readiness. How ready are the people within the organization and how will changes affect them? Like operational readiness, there is a need to quantify how prepared our company and employees are before go-live. This could be done in several different ways.

One way might be to go through scenarios of user acceptance testing. Maybe we host conference room pilots. However we choose to explore this, it's key to measure how well people understand those business processes before throwing them in the water and expecting them to swim. In other words, the business processes and the systems may work from a technical perspective, but we need to ensure that our employees understand how those processes work. It is essential to demonstrate some level of competency in performing those processes within the new system *before* going live with the software and risking operational disruption.

Our business case should include metrics that measure the percentage of the organization that has been fully trained and has demonstrated competency in performing end-to-end business processes in the new normal. We need to keep a pulse on progress and be able to easily identify the employees and teams that need more attention through the transformation project.

Operational Risk

In any high-ticket business investment, it's foolish to not measure the risks that come with the pursuit. What happens if, during go-live, not only are the expected business benefits not achieved but basic operations are also disrupted? What is the magnitude of that potential disruption or deviation from expected benefits? This is something we likely don't want to measure, but there is a need to identify and quantify the level of tolerance a company can handle at any given point of the project.

For example, if a shipping and fulfillment company goes live with new software, but the orders stop coming through and shipments cease, their whole business will fall flat until they can get back up and running. If the orders can't be shipped for a certain amount of time, say five days, they'd have to determine whether or not that is an acceptable delay.

Again, if we do everything right during the transformation and are following best practices throughout, this becomes less of an issue. Even so, preparing for those risks and delays is what will keep us afloat when faced with any type of operational disruption. Thinking through the potential risks could also help us determine things like timelines. Let's take Hershey's epic ERP failure as an example. After Hershey's suffered an SAP ERP failure, the company was incapable of processing $100 million worth of Kiss and Jolly Rancher orders, even though it had most of the inventory in stock.

Hershey's made a couple of textbook implementation mistakes in relation to project timing. The first is that they tried to squeeze a complex ERP implementation project into an unreasonably short timeline. This sacrificed their due diligence for the sake of expediency, and it set them up for ERP implementation trouble straight out the gate.

The second was a scheduling mistake. Hershey's timed its cutover during Halloween season – one of their busiest seasons. It was unreasonable for Hershey's to expect that it would be able to meet peak demand when its employees had not yet been fully trained on the new systems and workflows. Even in the best-case ERP implementation scenarios, companies should still expect performance declines because of the steep learning curves. The key is to shorten the learning curve and minimize disruption. Having that expectation in our back pocket will keep us from experiencing what Hershey's experienced. Be aware that there will be a slight (if we do it right) dip in operations at the time of go-live. The question is, what is a reasonable dip and what is the plan to get back into shape once it happens?

Business Value and ROI

The next performance metric to look at is business value and ROI, or return on investment. It is important to be thinking about how to *maximize* business value and get the full ROI out of the system or systems. An organization can quantify those expectations in the frame of inventory levels. We can optimize the system through better planning by reducing inventory or increasing revenue by a certain percentage using new sales enablement tools.

These are examples of things that might drive revenue enhancements, thus driving the ROI of the project. The question becomes, then, what do we expect the revenue enhancements to be? In general, it is imperative to evaluate business benefits and quantify them to ensure people are held accountable.

By incorporating these high-level metrics into the business case, we'll initiate the project from a calculated and intentional stance. Of course, we could always have more metrics that are specific to our industry and business, but these metrics are the non-negotiable elements that we must incorporate into the business plan. It will not only lay the groundwork for the digital transformation, but it will also serve as a tool to acquire full alignment from executives and the project team, alike.

But, what if the business case is questioned, there are uncertainties around the efficiency measures that were taken, or leaders don't agree on the functionality that is included in the business case? As the instigator of the digital transformation, the goal should always be alignment before anything else. To do that, we much go beyond the numbers.

Sometimes, the pushback will come in full force even when the numbers make sense. It's a big jump, and the larger the transformation proposal, the bigger the jump. It's natural to experience hesitation, and the wins and losses alike will always fall heaviest on an executive's shoulders. They may shy away from risks this big, and it's actually quite common. In these cases, it's time to put on our visionary hat and showcase a little extra boost to finalize the approval or alignment of a digital transformation.

Create a strong business case that not only draws alignment but acts as the differentiator between ERP failure or reaching the third stage of ERP success, or as I've been calling it, orbit. Consider the following ideas that paint the picture outside of the 'hard dollar' benefits, and take a more visionary approach to speak the same language as other executives.

Support of Strategic Vision

Most companies have some version of longer-term visions that align with the overarching corporate strategy – things like global consolidation and standardization, new market entry, changes to an acquisition structure, etc. While it is hard to tie dollars to technology investment on a future vision that may still be in the making, an appropriate technology platform could help to pave the way.

Take, for instance, a beverage company considering future vertical integration of its supply chain. There are many points to consider and many ways this could look, but having a system that can handle a variety of manufacturing processes could turn out to be a huge advantage. Outlining the path that will get the business from its current state to its future state through the use of technology will not only make the business case more cohesive, but it could also speak the love language of the person who needs a bit more convincing.

Cultural Alignment

One of the greatest, yet overlooked, aspects of software during an evaluation is the cultural alignment between the software's functionalities and our company's culture. If one of the pillars to a company's success comes by quickly adapting to meet customer demand, then the selected software should also mirror that cultural nuance. An example of this would be a company that thrives on implementing rigid changes that hold across its global locations, or even having the autonomy for localized departments to set their own processes. These are examples of cultural specifications that can either be amplified or dimmed depending on the type of technology selected.

This specification can be challenging to measure and outline, but it is an area of opportunity that all executives are, or should be, mindful of. The existing landscape of an organization may have a manipulated system in place to work as needed, but there could be benefits in acquiring a system that accepts the level of adaptability that fits and expands on the company's culture.

Market Image

If we are a publicly-traded company, it goes without saying that others are watching our technology investments. Some moves can even sway the stock price. However, even privately-held firms may see benefits in the image that a new system creates. Here are a few scenarios to consider.

Scenario #1: Credibility

When vendors and customers get word that technology investment is underway, it may help provide validation that we are a profitable company and are taking steps to better business relationships.

Scenario #2: Valuation

If we are in a position to be acquired, our ERP technology in place will be a very significant factor in valuation. We will need to consider the value increase of newer, more robust software versus the cost savings of a smaller, more limited solution. It is important to understand what private equity firms want from digital transformation. We strongly recommend bringing in experts to help evaluate this decision and the long vs. short-term benefits of both directions.

Scenario #3: Acquisition Confidence

If we are considering an acquisition and are in a competitive bidding situation, technology could be in our favor. The technology we have in place may help sway a decision pending impact on the acquired firm.

Scenario #4: User Satisfaction

Users cannot be overlooked as they will ultimately be the ones that drive the benefit of a new system. Even if we are not able to show significant ROI on a new system from an efficiency savings standpoint, replacing an old, unfavored system with one that has a better user interface or provides an easier work environment, then this could define a win. It may also help human resources with hiring younger workers. This would ultimately drive actual, measurable benefits in more ways than a monetary ROI.

Typically, the purpose of a business case is to provide justification for a digital transformation, outlining the details of the project and ultimately determining the ROI that can be achieved by moving forward. However, it's important to reposition our perspective of what a business case can do. It can be much more than an initial tool for approval. Aside from what was discussed above, let's now explore how to draft a *strong* business plan.

Make sure your business case is accurate and realistic.

Understanding the total cost of ownership is key. Look beyond the quote from prospective software vendors. Will there be other costs indirectly related to the actual software integration? Some examples could be backfilling internal resources, upgrading infrastructure, and hiring a third party to customize the technology. There is usually so much more behind the curtain than the original quote we receive. It takes big-picture thinking to dial in on what it will take to see success across the board. This is the most important piece, as it will help us determine a true ROI for our project.

Identify the benefits that will be realized as a result of the transformation.

Evaluate what the right technology can do for our organization. There are incredible benefits that come from successfully implementing a new ERP system and it's important to highlight the true benefits that will be applicable to our company's production. If we are in the manufacturing industry, we could cut costs through inventory reduction and transparency in everything from raw materials to production statuses. If we're looking at improving sales, the right system could help close more business and drive top-line revenue growth for the company.

There are also many intangible benefits to integrating new systems ranging from enhanced customer experience to increased employee retention due to new transparency and simplicity across the organization.

Provide project governance through the full transformation.

This element of a business case is oftentimes the most overlooked segment, and arguably one of the most important. Of course, we all will set goals and objectives, but approaching this piece as a pillar that will aid in future decision-making is key. At some point during the project, an executive or other team members may want to alter the original plan. Their request may be to add a new module or even customize a segment of the software. If our business case has well-defined goals and objectives, then it can act as a guide for business decisions along the way. It can serve as the map to help the team determine whether or not the request will move the needle toward the overarching goals and objectives of the project.

Companies that utilize a business case often see more success in their transformations than those that don't for this exact reason. It's easy to get distracted as new capabilities are discovered as the project progresses. Project governance acts as a guardrail to keep the project from getting off course, and a business case can act as a project governance tool.

Align your Organizational Change Management strategy with your business case.

The framework set around the project's goals and objectives of the project must also outline the organizational change management strategy for go-live. How will roles be redesigned to fit the new system? Will there be portions of the business that will have to reinvent the way they operate? The areas of impact and the magnitude of organizational change should be listed in our business case. Once identified, the business case can act as a roadmap to implementing specific training and communication plans for those departments or roles impacted by the changes.

Incorporate a benefits realization plan.

Dialing in on the key metrics stated in the previous pages will enable the project team to measure the success of a project. It will help determine the success factors of the project, and be the speedometer for the progress of the digital transformation. It will also create focus and accountability within the team, ensuring everyone is doing their part to support a successful IT transformation.

By tracking hard numbers and data as it relates to the progression of software implementation, we will be able to better recognize where we are achieving the benefits and where we may be falling short post software integration. Understanding the areas we are falling short could help determine the reasoning and, more importantly, the solution to turn it from red to green.

The good news is that it's often simple fixes. Many times, things can be course corrected by providing more training for a particular workgroup, reconfiguring the software to fit the need better, or simply cleaning up the data entering the system. Relatively speaking, these fixes are daily, small-scale, and easily attainable to help close open ends of the project. It's when key processes are not measured that things get missed and opportunities to improve are lost.

To summarize, the purpose of a business case is to outline a plan to achieve benefits associated with an optimized technology. By building a case that addresses all three pillars of transformation – people, processes, and technology – the business case will not only sell the project to decision-makers, but it will be a means for project governance that carries the investment through and helps make a significant, positive impact on the organization as a whole. When we align the numbers, the plan, and the vision together, we'll usually have a very compelling case for change.

Chapter 20

Top Existing and Emerging Technologies in the Digital Era

Each morning we wake up, there are new breakthroughs and discoveries within the technology industry. Through this continuous evolution, we will bear witness to the creation of new, innovative, emerging technologies and the revamp of existing technologies. When it comes time to truly consider the best software solutions for our organization, it's helpful to have a pulse on what is out there.

There are a plethora of options to choose from. From leading ERP systems, such as SAP and Oracle, to best-of-breed solutions that focus on more specific practices like human resources, sales, or supply chain management. There are countless avenues we can go down when it comes to software selection. So, how do we know which is the best software for our organization? Well, it depends…

Various ERP software options have distinct strengths, weaknesses, pros, cons, and tradeoffs. Depending on our company size, industry, geography, and strategic objectives, different systems will have different rankings. Simply put, ERP software can't be everything to everyone, so there are inherent tradeoffs depending on the company's specific needs.

With this in mind, a good starting point is to review the top solutions on the market and determine what might be the best fit. Based on independent experience, research, and database tracking, the strengths and weaknesses of all major enterprise systems in the market, my company, Third Stage Consulting Group, has developed a ranking methodology that compares general functionality, ease of adoption, flexibility, integration, average time and cost to implement, size of customer install base, product maturity, and a variety of other criteria. Once you put this book down, you can visit Third Stage Consulting's website for more specific product reviews and updated rankings each year. Until then, let's walk through the list of the most effective software solutions out there. It's important to note that there is no bias or special interest in listing these software solutions, but rather a comprehensive knowledge and experience base with each of these solutions that have proven to be effective for my previous clients. The following provides a summary of some of these rankings for a number of different scenarios.

General Ranking of the Best ERP Software

A high-level ranking is always a good place to start when beginning software evaluations. This ranking is a general comparison of all the leading ERP systems in the market. It's not segmented by industry, company size, geography, or any specific business need, so it is a broader and more general ranking of systems (in no particular order). This chart shows the system movement from 2022 – 2024 as well as "Top Selected Systems".

> **10.** Force (9)
> **9.** Odoo (8, 10th most selected)
> **8.** Oracle NetSuite (2, 2nd most selected)
> **7.** IFS (IFS (5, 7th most selected))
> **6.** SAP S/4HANA (4, 4th most selected)
> **5.** Epicor (new, 5th most selected)
> **4.** Workday (new)
> **3.** Infor CloudSuite (6, 3rd most selected)
> **2.** Oracle Fusion ERP Cloud (3, 6th most selected)
> **1.** Microsoft D365 F&O (1, #1 most selected)

Best ERP Software for Small Business

Small and mid-size businesses have unique needs that set them apart from other organizations. For example, they generally value flexibility and ease of implementation more so than their larger counterparts. For this reason, small businesses often find a different set of ERP systems to be more suitable for their needs (in no particular order).

Odoo

Microsoft Dynamics Business Central

Oracle NetSuite

Deacom

Epicor

Quickbooks

Salesforce / Financial Force

SAP Business One

Priority Software

Sage ERP

Best ERP Software for Large Businesses

Small businesses typically value speed, flexibility, cost, and other priorities that align with their goals and objectives. Larger organizations, on the other hand, tend to value the ability of ERP software to scale, standardize, and integrate across disparate parts of the business. For this reason, larger organizations typically pursue very different short-lists than those of their smaller counterparts.

Organizations such as Fortune 1000 businesses, multinational corporations, and state and federal governments are more likely to evaluate a markedly different short-list of ERP vendors. Below are the most commonly pursued ERP systems for larger organizations (in no particular order):

SAP S/4HANA

Oracle ERP Cloud

Microsoft Dynamics 365 Finance and Operations

Workday

Deltek

Best ERP Software for Manufacturing and Distribution Businesses

Manufacturers face unique needs and criteria when evaluating their ERP software options. In addition to software that can automate their manufacturing shop floors, manufacturing and distribution businesses typically value systems that can help with product lifecycle management, demand forecasting, advanced planning, job costing, and other differentiating requirements (in no particular order).

IFS

QAD

IQMS

SAP S/4HANA

Oracle ERP Cloud

Microsoft Dynamics 365

Infor CloudSuite

Epicor

Plex Systems

Deacom

Acumatica

Best ERP Software for Government and Non-Profit Organizations

State, federal, local, and national government agencies have unique needs as well. Their focus on fund accounting, budgeting, asset management, and other functions typically leads them down different paths than their private company counterparts. The same goes for non-profits.

DelTek

Netsuite

Oracle PeopleSoft

WorkDay

Oracle ERP Cloud

Sage Intacct

Infor Lawson

SAP S/4HANA

Microsoft Dynamics 365

Unit4

Best ERP Software for Best of Breed Digital Transformations

Regardless of our industry, organization size, or geography, it may be that a big, single ERP system is not the best fit. Instead, we may benefit more from a best-of-breed ERP system – in other words, pursuing different technologies for different parts of our business. Human capital management (HCM) software, customer relationship management (CRM) software, and supply chain management (SCM) technologies are some of the most common best-of-breed options. Here are a few in no particular order.

Top CRM Systems

Hubspot CRM

Oracle CRM Cloud

SalesForce

Microsoft Dynamics CRM

Top HCM Systems

Workday

SAO SuccessFactors HCM Suite

Oracle HCM Cloud

Top SCM Systems

Infor CloudSuite or Nexus

Oracle ERP Cloud or SCM Cloud

Plex Systems

Oracle NetSuite

These software solutions are just some of the options we should consider in our quest to find the best ERP software for our unique organization. At times, we tend to get boxed into a corner, thinking that these enterprise solutions are our only options. The reality is that there are a lot of newer, emerging technologies that have sprouted in recent years that could be the best solution for our organization's needs.

These emerging technologies may bend and even break the ideologies that software vendors what to instill. Big software companies will often try to be everything to everyone and tell us that we might fail if we go in a different direction. At the end of the day, we know our needs better than anyone. As long as we do our due diligence and understand our corporate vision as it relates to our digital strategy, we will know which route is best for us.

As we evaluate the bigger, more well-known software vendors out there, it's also important to evaluate the advantages and disadvantages of emerging and customized software solutions on the market as well. Let's walk through those options and discuss what our options are outside of the basic ERP solution.

Emerging Technologies

Hyper-Focused Best of Breed Supply Chain Management Solutions

For a lot of organizations, SCM is a critical function. In the early 2020s, supply chain challenges and pitfalls were exposed as companies navigated manufacturing and distribution disruptions from the pandemic. With that came ample learnings and reprioritization of supply chain management efforts. There has been an uptick in the adoption of supply chain-focused technologies and a greater push into automation as it relates to supply chain functionality.

In the lists of ERP solutions above, we covered a handful of enterprise technologies that specialize exclusively in maintaining and managing a supply chain. However, we can go beyond the typical SCM systems listed above. There are relatively new, niche systems such as warehouse management software, procurement systems, logistics, shipping, and freight management solutions that organizations are implementing to increase efficiencies across distinct elements of their operations. Many of these micro-focused systems can perform at a higher level than a larger ERP solution that has a supply chain functionality.

Machine Learning and Robotics Process Automation

Machine learning and RPA are different technologies, but they are similar in the sense that they are leveraged to automate and predict common or mundane processes that humans typically perform. Take, for example, invoice processing. By integrating one of these solutions, we would be able to automate the process of paying invoices. The system would sort and pay invoices, flagging any that seem off or fall out of a distinct pattern.

Both machine learning and RPA are able to tackle a simple business process and open up more time for people to focus on tasks that require a greater need for human reasoning. There are stand-alone machine learning and RPA systems on the market, but some of the larger ERP vendors are beginning to incorporate these technologies as a part of their overarching service. When evaluating our options, we should consider what this type of technology can do for our production levels, as well as for our organization's scalability.

Business Process Mining Tools

There are tools, like Celonis, for example, that help define and highlight what is truly happening within business processes and systems. As discussed in Part I, business process mining quantifies and analyzes different steps in the workflow. We can start to identify and quantify where breakdowns are happening and where there are variations in a specific process. It delivers quantitative data to augment that qualitative tribal knowledge that many organizations have been built upon.

Employee Adoption Tools

Employee adoption tools may be a great investment if we plan to undergo a digital transformation in the near future. These technologies are meant to train employees on business processes and workflows, providing tutorials and 'how-to's' as an employee goes from one activity to the next. Start with the existing software provider and see if they have an employee adoption tool built into their system. Some systems have this embedded into their platform to provide a tutorial or step-by-step guide for a specific user. There are also independent employee adoption tools that can be used across various systems.

Open Source and Low Code Software

Open source software, such as Odoo, uses a common programming language. With that common programming language, organizations with an adept IT team can easily change the software and enable it to do what the organization needs it to do. On the other side of the coin, we have low-code software that allows us to change workflows and user interfaces without having to change the main source code.

Low code requires less technical competency, and open source needs more technical competency. If our organization has the talent needed to facilitate the technical capabilities to support it, then open-source systems may be our best bet.

Custom Development and Application

Although this isn't necessarily an emerging technology, it's an option that many seem to have forgotten still exists. Organizations may need custom software that they can often develop in-house. By going this route, the open-ended areas of existing solutions can be customized by developing their own applications.

This is especially important if there are specific differentiators that serve us as a competitive advantage. We don't necessarily need to fit in off-the-shelf software, even though the software vendors on the shelf will tell us otherwise. Many organizations benefit from having a custom-fit solution that caters to their distinct needs.

As we begin indulging in the technical aspect of our digital transformation, it's helpful to wrap our minds around the catalog of options we have when it comes to selecting software. Although there are hundreds of solutions available, our digital strategy and the work we have done up to this point will guide us in dialing down on a short-list of solutions. Once we have a short-list, the entire software evaluation process becomes much more digestible. The question remains – how do we build a short-list?

Chapter 21

Which Software is Right for You?

I want to take a moment and highlight the fact that we are nearly at the end of the book, and we are just now getting started on the tangible implementation of technology. This is important to be cognizant of. The fact of the matter is that for a digital transformation to be successful, most of the work takes place before we even consider software. Why? Well, it's simple. The software selection process is one of the first, tangible steps related to implementing technology that can make or break our digital transformation.

There are so many software solutions on the market that selecting the right one is a daunting challenge without proper preparation. However, if we know the intricacies of the company's needs, wants, prioritized processes, and cultural nuances, then it becomes much easier to dial in on the right software selection. We will take everything up to this point in the book, and we will funnel it into developing a short-list of viable software solutions that can move the needle for our organization.

Thorough software evaluations across a short-list of options are imperative, and it's important to understand the overarching capabilities and functionalities of each software before we marry our operations to one system. Being thoughtful during each step of the selection process can make or break our transformation as a whole, with each step relying on the steps before it.

Before comparing software side by side, we need to have the following checked off our to-do list.

- We've dialed in on the processes and operations that need TLC.
- We've figured out the people who will be working on the project and sharing their inputs along the way.
- We've found an executive sponsor for the project.
- We've acquired alignment across all executives and stakeholders.

- We've determined where we will turn to ask clarifying questions on how to optimize the specifics of a process.
- We've outlined the timeline and goals of the digital transformation project.
- We have aligned those goals with the overarching mission of the organization.
- We've determined the upstream and downstream effects of the organizational change.
- We clearly understand our competitive landscape and know what we need to do to become more competitive.
- We've dialed in on the needs vs. wants of our organization, prioritizing the processes that need to be improved upon.

Once we can confidently say that we have done all of these things, we are ready to start shopping for software. Here, we will create a blueprint of sorts for the hypothetical implementation of our software, and apply the hypothetical across divisional operations to get an overarching idea of what implementation will look like. This way, we can both zoom in and zoom out to see the most minute details in conjunction with the bigger picture.

There will be areas of focus depending on our type of organization, and it's alright to not hit each nail right on the head. Categorize and prioritize when considering software — what must go, what could go, and what should stay. Of course, this doesn't have to be a firm and set-in-stone plan for our transformation. Rather, it's a malleable framework to guide the process. This is the starting point of the selection process and is what initially defines our implementation plan.

Selecting the Best-Fit Software: 4 Milestones of Software Evaluations

Become crystal clear on prioritized processes.

The first thing to do when it comes time to evaluate systems is to revisit our process. More specifically, we'll revisit the *Hierarchy of Business Processes* we reviewed in Part I. As a refresher, it's all about process mapping and prioritizing our processes by placing them in a hierarchy. The hierarchy has five levels, with commodity processes landing at level one and core competencies landing at level five. Levels two and three are when the type of

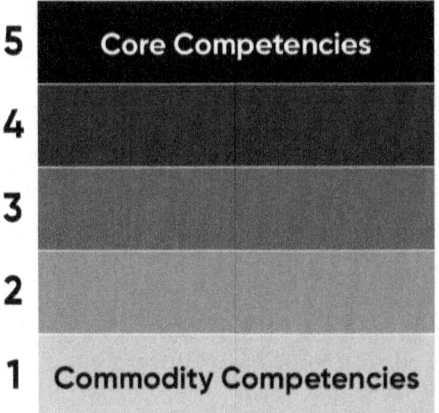

Core Competencies: These are the things that make us who we are as an organization. It's why we win against the competition, what we do well and what we want to continue to do well.
Examples: Processes that are either customer-facing, employee experience-based, or product-based. It's the things that we tailor and customize to make our organization unique. Without them, we'd lose our edge and our brand would fall flat.

Commodity Competencies: These are things like accounts payable or purchase order processing. It's what all organizations must do, and there are similar processes in place from company to company.
Examples: Processes that don't need customization because they're meant to be generic, and they're efficient being so.

technology we leverage starts to matter in regards to keeping the integrity of our prioritized processes. Let's revisit this concept.

When evaluating commodities processes at level one, nearly all technology can get the job done. Nearly all ERP solutions will have high-quality accounts payable and receivables functionalities. They will all be able to pull a balance sheet. They will all be able to do the rudimentary tasks that are pertinent to the back-office operations of our organization. It's when we get to customer service processes or production processes that things become more complex.

While we can defer the processes in level one to the software, by level five, our processes should be driving the technology. The core competencies are the most high-priority and high-value of our processes, and we need to figure out a way for the technology to support these processes, not the other way around.

Dial in on a short-list of viable software solutions.

Once we have the set processes and functionalities that we want to compare software solutions to, we will have a laundry list of software to evaluate. The goal here is to narrow down this long list to a short-list of about six to ten different software solutions. In order to build a strong short-list, consider evaluating the following elements of each software vendor.

- Marketing efforts
- Market reviews
- User feedback
- Substance behind the brand's messaging

User feedback will vary from company to company. There will be some people that love it, and there will be some people that hate it. The key here is to get an idea of what kind of companies are using what software. It will help us get a better understanding of which ones would be applicable to our organization. Keep this step surface level. If we go as far as to reach out to each and every company on our long list, we'll be inundated and overwhelmed with their follow-up sales team. Poke around the web to find information independently, and drop vendors with the lowest ratings and feedback. Take note of the ones that stand out, and move on to the next step.

With six to ten names on our narrowed-down list, it's now time to dive deeper. It's time to investigate. It's time to reach out to the software vendor and start digging. Here are a handful of questions to keep top of mind as we explore and evaluate the software solutions on our short-list.

- How is the customer experience and how do they handle their customer's needs?
- When these companies route calls, do they both answer and have a general understanding of the questions you're asking? In other words, is their customer service team attentive and competent?
- Ask any high-level questions to get more familiar with the software vendor's brand. What they portray on the surface will shine a light on what is beneath the hood and what a potential partnership with them could look like.
- Ask for scripted demonstrations to make sure your requirements can be met with their software.

Now, we are getting a clearer picture of which software vendors we feel drawn to and which ones can take a back seat. With each step, our list will likely get smaller and smaller. At this point, we might have three to six software vendors that we are still considering. Let's get onto the next consideration: System architecture.

The key here is understanding integration points between systems. At this step in the process, all we need to do when it comes to integration with other systems currently in use is to familiarize ourselves with exactly which team members we'll be working with to integrate the new technology. We simply need to get ducks in a row to ensure our team has the background and capabilities to help us through the transformation once the time comes for implementation and integration of the new system with the existing systems. The ticket here is communication. This is where change management sets into play. All stakeholders, including those who are managing a separate software within the company, should be queued in on what's coming down the pipeline. No one wants to be blindsided.

The software selection process can be daunting when we realize just how many solutions there are on the market. When evaluating software for a digital transformation, it's important to analyze the strategy required more so than the ins and outs of the products themselves. A software selection should also be made with an eye on the future, as the software will ideally outlast the digital transformation it was chosen to support. Let's take a hypothetical case study of a digital transformation.

Preserving the Engineering Culture: A Global ERP Implementation Case Study

This case study explores how a medical device manufacturer, operating across six continents with headquarters in New Zealand, successfully replaced its outdated ERP system to accommodate its expanding global operations. The company's strong engineering-focused culture and "do it our way" mentality posed unique challenges during the ERP selection and implementation process. The study outlines the steps taken to ensure the preservation of the engineering culture while transitioning to SAP S/4HANA as the new global ERP solution.

The medical device manufacturer in focus is a leading company in the production and distribution of breathing devices. With a robust annual revenue of $500 million and a presence on six continents, the organization faced mounting challenges as its existing 30-year-old ERP system, which was heavily customized, could no longer meet the demands of its growing global operations. To maintain its core corporate culture of engineers creating value for patients and foster innovation, the company decided to embark on a comprehensive ERP replacement project while ensuring minimal disruption to ongoing operations.

The company initiated the Third Stage project with the primary objective of selecting a suitable ERP system that would support its global operations and align with its engineering-centric culture. The project team conducted selection activities across its various global sites, engaging stakeholders from different functional areas. A series of process improvement workshops and demonstrations were organized to gather feedback from users, understand pain points, and identify specific ERP requirements.

After an extensive evaluation process, the project team selected SAP S/4HANA as the preferred ERP solution. The choice of SAP S/4HANA was based on its ability to provide a robust and scalable platform that could accommodate the company's growing needs, coupled with its reputation for driving organizational efficiency.

The engineering-focused corporate culture of the company was a vital aspect that the project team aimed to maintain during the ERP implementation. Recognizing the strong "do it our way" mentality, the team developed a tailored implementation strategy that involved extensive collaboration with the engineering teams. The objective was to integrate their expertise and unique requirements into the ERP system to ensure a seamless transition.

To minimize resistance to change and enhance overall ERP adoption, the project team conducted focus groups and organizational readiness assessments. These initiatives allowed the team to identify potential challenges and address concerns that may arise during the implementation process.

Feedback from employees was incorporated into the project plan, which resulted in a more cohesive and harmonious transition.

To mitigate risks and maintain steady operations, the company opted for a phased global rollout of SAP S/4HANA by functional area. This approach ensured that each department and region had sufficient time to adapt to the new system while allowing for fine-tuning based on early feedback. It also allowed for valuable knowledge transfer between the teams involved in different phases of the rollout.

Results and Benefits: The successful implementation of SAP S/4HANA as the global ERP system yielded several benefits for the medical device manufacturer:

1. Enhanced Efficiency: The new ERP system streamlined processes, reducing redundant tasks and automating various operations, resulting in increased overall efficiency.

2. Improved Global Collaboration: SAP S/4HANA facilitated seamless collaboration among global teams, enabling better sharing of information and resources.

3. Better Data Visibility: The ERP system provided real-time data insights, empowering decision-makers to make informed choices based on accurate and up-to-date information.

4. Preserved Engineering Culture: By involving the engineering teams throughout the implementation process, the company ensured that its core culture of innovation and value creation remained intact.

By strategically planning the project and involving stakeholders from different functional areas, the organization achieved a smooth and phased global rollout, ensuring minimal disruption to operations while embracing a more advanced ERP solution. The project's success demonstrated the company's commitment to maintaining its engineering culture and its dedication to continual improvement and innovation in the medical device industry.

Tips to consider before making a software decision.

Get to know the software on a deeper level.

When evaluating ERP systems, the vendor demonstration process is a complete waste of time. In doing this for 20-plus years, we found that those demos don't necessarily give us an inaccurate picture of what the software can and can't do. There's almost always a disconnect between what we see in demos, what products can actually do, and how those products might actually fit our organization.

One of the advantages of being a sales representative for an ERP or HCM software vendor is that they get advanced versions of software to showcase in a demonstration. What we see at the demo table is the premium version of the solution. As a matter of fact, when it comes to demonstrations, vendors will not show much of the software at all. Instead, they're showing PowerPoint screenshots on their local machine. Many times, they're not even accessing the cloud version of the software.

Sales representatives have a number of tools at their disposal that may or may not be reflective of the software that we'd actually be purchasing. As long as we are cognizant of that fact, then we will be less likely to fall prey to shiny-object syndrome.

The second problem with ERP vendor product demos is that they're biased. The software sales representative is speaking through the lens of how great their solutions are rather than what is truly best for our organization. The reason? What we buy as a company is directly linked to how big their wallets become. They want to show all the bells and whistles, cool functionalities, and the great advancements that have been made in artificial intelligence and machine learning.

The process intends to show us what the product can do and what it can do well so that we buy the most expensive version of the software. Many times, organizations don't need that. It'd be most helpful if demonstrations showcased what a software cannot do. That's arguably the more important part when it comes to evaluating a software solution. But, we all know that is not the best approach to sales.

Something that is rarely talked about in the vendor demonstration process is the inconsistent qualifications and capabilities of the sales representatives themselves. Occasionally, we'll see products that we know aren't a great fit for a client, but the sales representative is good at what they do. They only show the great strengths of the product and overstate the benefits for that particular organization. It's skewed, and if we are not careful, we won't be able to see the full picture.

In other cases, we may get a terrible sales representative who's selling a great product, but they completely bombed the main demonstration. They're unprepared and don't understand our business and don't have configured demos that are specific to our needs. They end up failing and we could end up passing on a system that may be a great fit for us. This is a lose/lose for everybody.

Now, although I just bashed the idea of sitting through product demonstrations, I'm not suggesting that we shouldn't do demos at all. But, if that's our primary focal point for our evaluation and the number one thing we base our decision on, we're making a big mistake.

I would, at best, treat it as one of several data points we use in evaluating software options and making decisions on our ERP or HCM product. Look at it this way – the data points that can be even more beneficial than a demo itself are things like quantitative ratings of how the system is actually being used.

Those data points become an objective way to look at how different systems in the marketplace stack up side-by-side against our criteria as an organization, all without the sales spin. Here is the bottom line, it's critical to get past that sales rhetoric and get quantitative and objective data. Why do I say that? Not all requirements, needs, and evaluation criteria are going to be equal, nor should they be equal.

It is important to prioritize and weigh the different decision criteria we're going to evaluate so that we can quickly narrow the field and focus on the most important criteria for our business, not necessarily what the software vendor wants to show us.

Here are a few basic considerations to get the most out of a software demonstration:

- If you are going to sit through demonstrations, try not to spend too much time on them. Some demonstrations could go as long as two to three days for a single ERP system. That's too much time.
- If you get to the point where you're wanting demos to last more than a full day per product, then you're getting into analysis paralysis and probably evaluating things that aren't or shouldn't be material to your decision process.
- If you are doing demos, take it with a grain of salt, limit the time you spend on it, and just use it as one of many data points in your overall evaluation process.
- If you come out of the demo feeling like the software can do everything you want it to do, something's wrong. There is no *one* fit solution. There is a *best fit* solution.

In the end, we can use the demo process as a means to validate that a software vendor is a good fit for us, but do not only rely on product demonstrations when making a decision. Remember to poke holes in the product and find pieces that may *not* be a good fit as well. This is just as important as what the system can do and how it can fit our capabilities and needs. Choose wisely.

Consider the return on investment

When selecting software, we will need to weigh the cost of implementation and of model and system procurement against the benefits. Now that we are down to just a few software solutions, we have the pricing and we have the scope of the functionalities. We must now consider the ROI of each solution. When thinking about implementation, consider the impact on our hardware and system infrastructure, both technologically and fiscally. Some other concerns over cost may include our timeline, data migration, data security, or the unavoidable fact that the bigger the transformation, the higher the overall risk.

A digital transformation is often a 'high risk, high reward' scenario. Regardless of how big of a bite we choose to take, we want to make sure it can be comfortably attained in our set budget. We don't want to cut corners, so we should pay for what we need, and only what we need, by considering both long-term and short-term implications and prioritizing what's important. While working through these tips and best practices, remember these last and final tips for evaluating and selecting the best software for our business and its organizational needs:

• Revisit your digital strategy to ensure that the software under consideration will deliver on the greater goals and objectives set forth at the beginning of the project.

- Match your software to critical requirements and key differentiators.
- Don't waste time on non-essential requirements.
- Price is rarely the most important differentiator so don't let it be the only determining factor.
- Define and validate a business case
- Look for the best fit for software, not the perfect fit
- Don't get caught up in "best practices".
- Don't overlook a software's cultural fit within your organization.
- Prioritize organizational change management to make sure your team adopts the new software and new processes with ease.

As companies increasingly look to digital transformation to help them compete in the modern economy and improve operational efficiency, dialing in on the right software selection becomes critical. With so many options on the market and so much at stake, the process of selecting the best system to fulfill a business's unique needs can be complicated and full of potential failure points.

Oftentimes, those failure points identify themselves through the process. If we've done everything stated in this book to the T, then these common red flags likely won't appear. If they do, then we need to take a time out, pause, and reassess. The key to success is having the humility and agility to course correct.

Whether we're looking to implement an all-encompassing ERP system or a focused best-of-breed system, it's important to understand the common red flags. When it comes to the software selection phase of a digital

🚩 transformation, these specific red flags will tell us whether or not we are making the right decision or not. Let these warning signs be triggers to pause the selection process and reevaluate what needs to be done to course correct.

Lack of overall strategy and digital roadmap

Selecting or implementing software can be one of the most expensive and resource-heavy transformations that a business goes through. Without a clear digital roadmap of how the organization will utilize a given software, the processes around it, and the implementation plan, the software will not deliver the maximum business value possible.

It's important to understand that a digital strategy is not just an operational strategy. We need to look at the business from a holistic point of view and understand our future state operating model in conjunction with our company culture. What will it take to evolve our processes and operations from what it is today to what it needs to be five to ten years from now? The software should help act as the bridge to get there. The only way to understand which software will be the best fit is to be a visionary and outline a thorough digital roadmap described in this book prior to moving forward with a software selection.

Going through the process of building and designing a digital strategy will also showcase the needs and requirements for a specific software system. It will make the selection process easier when we take our specific needs shopping with us to find the matching puzzle piece. As a reminder, there is no silver-bullet solution. There will never be one solution that solves every single pain point, so our decisions need to be led by our prioritized processes.

A cohesive digital roadmap or digital strategy needs to be in place before we can confidently select software. This information is going to be a playbook for our potential software selection and will help ensure we select a system that fully meets our needs as an organization.

Trusting vendor best practices

During the selection process, many software vendors will come to the table with 'proven best practices'. It's important to have some professional skepticism when evaluating such best practices. Keep in mind that strategies should be unique to the organization that is selecting the software, and what might be a best practice for one organization may be a nuisance for the next. Falling victim to these 'best practices' will not only cause the organization to lose ownership of the project, but it will also let the ecosystem of the software lead the selection rather than letting the business's unique needs lead the selection.

There will be multiple 'best practices' that meet our needs as a business or industry. In fact, we can utilize vendors' best practices, but it should only be if they align with our own strategic goals as a business. We should be intentional about staying true to our own roadmap and digital strategy, no other vendor knows our organization's goals and objectives as well as we do. We should own our project. Simply letting vendors lead the way is going to put our business at risk and our transformation project in jeopardy. We'd ultimately be putting the vendor's needs ahead of our own.

Lack of key performance indicators or business case measurement

When we start a software selection process, we should be very clear on the different key performance indicators or metrics that we want to measure and see progress on once the software is implemented. As an organization, we must ask ourselves the following questions:

- Is the software giving us what we need as a unique organization?
- Does the cost-benefit realization make sense?

The key is to unpack what the software is and how it will address our unique needs. This is a simplistic process that can often be watered down with new trending technology or new automation and emerging technologies. This means that though functions like artificial intelligence, predictive analytics, and

🚩 machine learning may be very important for future state goals, they may not be what our business needs *today*. Having a deep understanding of the needs of the business vs. the wants of the business, ensuring that the software is achieving those needs and the spending makes sense for our business case are all critical if we want to achieve the maximum business value of the software we choose to invest in.

Lack of understanding of the total cost of a software selection investment

Understanding the total cost of a software system purchase and implementation is imperative to achieving a successful digital transformation. The total cost of ownership of a software system extends far beyond the main purchase price. Considerations such as database management, hardware management, implementation resources, customization services, licensing, software-as-a-subscription costs, and other aspects need to be outlined and understood.

Be crystal clear in expectations during the contracting phase. Engage legal advice and support as needed. There is such a thing as ERP and software-focused legal counsel that helps businesses negotiate with the big software vendors. We never have to take what we get when it comes to signing a software vendor's contract. We can always negotiate.

When it's all said and done and we've dialed in on which software solution we'd like to implement, it comes down to expectations. The gap between expectations and reality needs to be minuscule. To get there, it takes working with the software vendor and their greater team to ensure they can deliver on what they sold us. It also takes a deep sense of ownership in our own project rather than welcoming strong influence from third parties that may not be in alignment with our values, culture, and overall objectives.

One of the biggest reasons organizations find themselves in litigation due to a failed digital transformation is the misalignment of what was represented during the sales process and what is actually happening come go-live. Other times, there could also be a gap between what the cost was expected to be and what the cost actually was. Again, expectation vs. reality.

By following these recommendations and keeping an eye out for the common red flags, we will be able to minimize the gap between expectation and reality. When we can confidently probe each vendor on the short-list, do our due diligence, and maintain our independence and ownership through the process, we're bound to land on the best-fit software that will fill the need for our organization.

Chapter 22

Implementation Planning

Once the selection of the software is complete, it's time to piece everything together into an implementation plan, in other words, a digital transformation execution strategy. This roadmap will put all the puzzle pieces of our digital strategy together to create a feasible implementation action plan. Implementation planning is a critical step in the process that occurs after software selection but before designing software and go-live. The more time and money spent on this segment, the more successful and speedy the software implementation will be, ultimately reducing the cost of the overall project.

Once organizations realize their need to implement new technology, they tend to jump into a digital transformation without covering their bases before they begin. Whether the lack of planning is due to an abundance of excitement or a heavy lenience on the system integrator, jumping in without a plan for the technical implementation of the software will often lead to ERP failure. On the contrary, those who have a full-scope implementation plan are more likely to optimize their digital transformation and maximize their ROI through the process.

So, what is an implementation plan? Ultimately, it's everything that will get our software implementation from point A to point B. From building and configuring the software to fit our system architecture to the organizational change management tactics and strategies we plan to see through, an implementation plan should illustrate how we will proceed with the technical side of our digital transformation. It's a more technical view of our timelines, goals, and governance of the overarching process that was discussed at a higher level in the business case. In fact, we can pull from our business case in relevant areas to build a strong implementation plan.

The key to an effective implementation plan is to ensure the software vendor's plan is realistic for our organization. Oftentimes, software vendors, sales representatives, and system integrators will provide a proposed project plan that's unrealistic in scope and timelines. So, before we even dive into our own implementation planning process, we need to make sure there is a realistic implementation plan from the technical software providers as well.

Once we feel confident in what our software vendor brings to the table, we can begin the process of implementation planning. As we walk down this path, realize that this plan is all-encompassing. It holds much more than process improvement timelines. We must consider elements and aspects of all three pillars of digital transformation we have discussed in this book: *People, Processes, and Technology.*

That's right, this is the part where everything we have covered in this book comes together. What has been discussed up to this point is now going to be put into tangible action. Let's break down what that looks like.

Processes

Process mapping is a key element in creating an implementation plan. What will our business processes look like with the new technology we chose during the software selection process? What is our target operating model? What is our desired future state and how can technology help us get there? Now that we have completed *The Hierarchy of Business Processes*, we need to, quite literally, map out how our prioritized, level five processes flow from start to finish.

Consider what the process flow entails *today* and how we want them to flow once the new software is tied in. Once we have this piece dialed in, we can share the vision with a system integrator to bring it to fruition. First, we'll create a process map and perform a gap analysis to help identify where technology can bridge the gap from our current operations to our ideal, target operating model.

 *Refer to Part I: Processes, chapter 4 to refresh on process improvement best practices.*

As we evaluate existing processes, brainstorm new processes, and build a plan to get from one side of the canyon to the other, we must ask ourselves the following questions,

- What will our business processes look like with new technology?
- What is our target operating model?
- What is our desired future state and how can technology help us get there?

The answers to these three questions must be woven into the overarching implementation plan. It's critical that we have a good sense of how our processes flow from start to finish, and how we want them to flow with the implementation of new software.

People

It's only human nature that executives pull in different, and sometimes conflicting, directions. The head of sales will often have different goals and priorities than the head of procurement. A cohesive implementation plan will include a consensus using proven methodology and techniques to get executives to interact and commit to the same vision and the same priorities.

It's not an exaggeration to say that solid executive alignment is the exception rather than the norm. If misalignment is suspected, it's in our best interest to bring in an objective third-party consultant to help dial down on the root of the problem and drive everyone back to the same playing field. Whether it's done internally or externally, we must facilitate strategic orientation, engagement, and discussion where team members are forced to come out of their silos and collaboratively inch towards alignment. Knowing how to build successful outcomes and facilitate contentious faceoffs are some of the traits of an experienced strategy-based independent ERP consultant. That's what we should look for if we consider bringing in a third-party expert to help point all sails in the right direction.

Note that just because an executive approves the project does not necessarily mean all parties are aligned. The future state vision starts at the top, and that vision serves as the foundation of any digital transformation.

Executives should be crystal clear on the business goals and objectives of the company, and ultimately the purpose of implementing new software, and communicate that clearly with the project team. The executive and project team must consider what the end game looks like to ensure we are all acting and leading with the same intention.

Misalignment is far too often the culprit of trailing performance when it comes to new software implementation. With that said, executives should focus on the following three things to keep from falling prey to misalignment amongst themselves, and ultimately amongst their greater team.

- Executives should educate themselves to fully understand what the implementation means and what to expect. The more realistic the view executives can grasp, the better off they will be. This often comes with the feedback and insights garnered through the various organizational and procedural assessments.
- Executives should establish the guardrails that will keep the project aligned with overarching business goals, from start to finish. If the objectives of the project are defined from the beginning, it will help keep the whole executive team and the project team aligned as key decisions are made throughout the project.
- Executive alignment will need to trickle down to the rest of the organization through proper internal communications. There is a lot that goes into executive alignment, and the risk of misalignment could trickle down into all aspects of the project if the leaders of the organization don't get ahead of the rhetoric. Communications should start at the beginning of the digital transformation and focus on how everyone, from the company as a whole to each person, will benefit from the change.

Until the alignment is there, we would be better off waiting on implementation.

Organizational change management is another key element of our implementation planning efforts. It is both an art and a science. If we don't have executive alignment at the top, fostering adoption and alignment among the troops becomes next to impossible. While training can be part of an OCM strategy, we mustn't confuse it with the need for something more comprehensive. A top-tier executive will work to continually educate themselves and their team on the direct correlation between creating fluid and well-executed change management strategies and ERP success, simply because they know the impact that change has on people.

Because each business is unique, organizational change management initiatives must be tailored and able to change as needed depending on the needs of each business. It is, at the core, the act of blending new technology with living, breathing employees that have wants, needs, and fears. Therefore, there isn't one, all-encompassing solution for change adoption. One size does not fit all because all employees, team dynamics, and company cultures are different.

It's not unusual for an ERP initiative to initially be viewed as exciting, only to have some individuals succumb to fear before going live. We're talking psychology, management style, educational adeptness, economics, and a handful of other fields combined to facilitate the implementation of a new process or technology. It's much larger than meets the eye, and it all comes down to how well we can manage people. To some on our team, change management will be viewed as unnecessary, kumbaya-like activities. To others, it will be viewed as necessary activities to remain competitive as a company. It's up to us to acquire buy-in vertically and laterally across the organization, and that will only come with executive alignment and proper organizational change management initiatives discussed in Part II.

The concept of organizational change management is often overlooked due to its intangible weight. The problem is that overlooking organizational change management and failing to plan a change management strategy before jumping into a digital transformation is what, single-handedly, throws digital transformations off the rails. We must have a change management strategy in place before diving into software implementation just as we have an ERP strategy in place. These two elements work hand in hand to make up the bulk of a cohesive implementation plan. The bottom line is that our team will inevitably resist change. It doesn't matter the type of organization. The question is, how severe is the resistance and where are the pockets of resistance going to come from? The organizational readiness assessment will point us to the best-fitting OCM tactics we should leverage and map out in our implementation plan. From the organizational readiness assessment, we will derive a communication plan and a training plan, and we will align our change

 *Refer to Part II: People to refresh on the processes needed to create a strong organizational change management plan.*

management efforts with the greater initiatives at play. By doing so, we'll be able to dial in on the biggest areas of risk that we will be up against when it comes to employees adapting to or rejecting the new technology: People.

Technology

We are now arriving in uncharted territory concerning what we've discussed in this book. The *technology* arm of our implementation includes everything that it takes to integrate and implement the software we have selected. We must now consider data migration, system architecture, and integration between systems as we enter this phase of the project. Let's dive a bit deeper.

Technical Readiness

The capacity to which our IT team is ready will define our company's next step toward adopting new software. If we are going from a cloud solution to a more customizable system, then the transition will require more due diligence. Think about it – when leveraging a standard cloud system, we are heavily dependent on the software vendor to push out updates and provide strong cybersecurity measures. All we would be doing, in theory, is fitting our processes into a structured platform. We will have different needs as we upgrade our software systems, and we must consider whether or not our team is ready and capable of handling the new normal. It comes down to three things: talent, system architecture, and data flow.

When evaluating our technical readiness, we must determine if our existing IT department has the right skills to accommodate the technicalities we are migrating to. Maybe they do, maybe they don't. If they don't, we need to pinpoint the training and certifications the team will need in order to be ready for the shift. Another option is to hire new talent altogether. In either scenario, these things take time and resources and we must act on them now.

In addition to the readiness of our IT talent, our digital infrastructure will also play a big role in implementing a new system. Are our internal IT department and system architecture ready for a change? Better yet, are they equipped to handle the new needs of the chosen software?

Be realistic in this evaluation. To be realistic, we must fully grasp what system architecture entails. System architecture is one of the keys to digital transformation. Especially in today's environment, many businesses leverage a plethora of technology to optimize operations. If we think about all the different operations and technology that businesses need to succeed – CRM for sales, HCM for human resources, WMS for warehouse management, robotics on the shop floor, finance – countless technologies are interwoven together to improve business operations. It's the way these systems communicate and function synergistically that composes our system architecture.

The best way to think about system architecture is a visual representation of how the different systems in our organization come together. There are organizations out there that have upwards of 200+ systems in place, and they can't even name all of them. This is especially true with companies that undergo or have undergone various mergers and acquisitions over time. Whether we have five systems or hundreds of systems in place, it's important to understand what each system is and how we are currently bringing them together. Once we understand that, then we can look at the future state of our system architecture once a new system is plugged into the formula.

It's helpful to visualize this on paper. Take, for instance, the web of systems below.

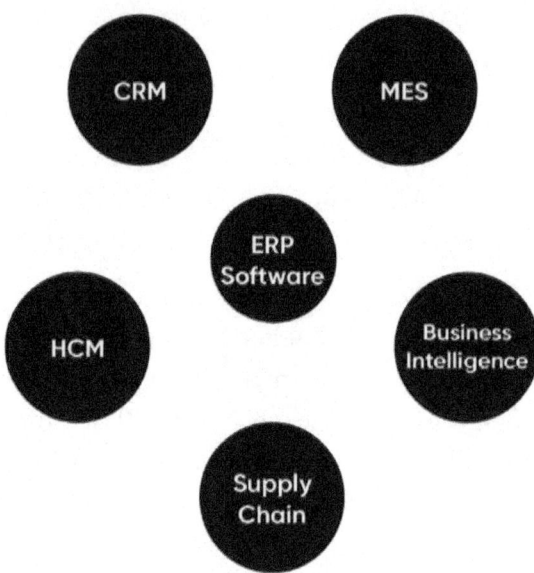

It often starts with a core ERP software as the center point, with smaller, best-of-breed software solutions that are connected to the core ERP solution. This web could expand out for miles depending on how many systems our organization has in place. To keep it simple, we will only look at a few common systems.

The first step is to look at how each software solution is integrated into the next. We must outline the system landscape and touchpoints. Start by connecting each system that currently speaks to each other.

Next, we must illustrate and highlight what dataflows are within each system. Let's start in the sales process. A deal is closed and now the salesperson is owed a commission. The commission is captured in the sales system which will connect back to the ERP system as a liability of sales commission to that salesperson. As a result of those commissions, we have something that needs to tie into payroll. The human capital management system will be fed that data from the ERP system. If we're a manufacturing company, then the ERP system might trigger another step in the process that starts an order with the MES system.

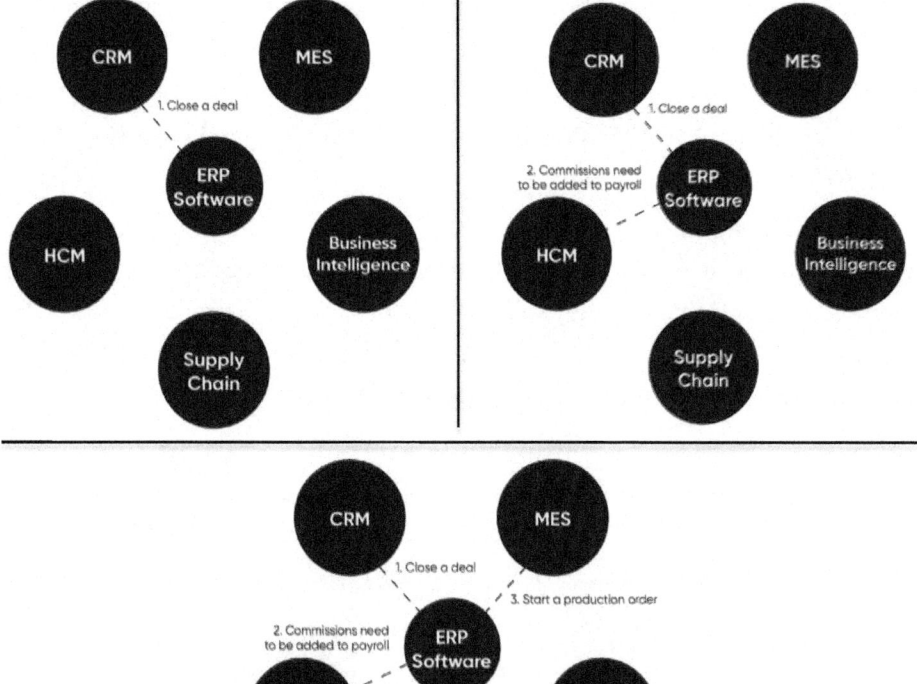

Each line that connects the systems is an integration point. Each integration point is critical to our new software implementation. This is one example of how one process can touch multiple systems. This architecture may look different between the current state and the future state depending on how large the digital transformation project is. It may be as simple as swapping out one of the best-of-breed systems, or it may be the implementation of a new ERP system that will need countless new integration points. If we look at multiple transactions across all the end-to-end processes of an organization, the diagram can become very large and complex.

The purpose of mapping out our system architecture is to understand how data flows between systems. When we do this, we can determine where the master data resides. When there are multiple systems, we run the risk of having mismatched data across each system. The key is to identify where the source of *truth* lies. We could decide that the ERP system is what houses the primary, master data, that feeds the rest of the systems. This will enable cleaner, more organized data flow across all our operations.

We are living in the era of big data. Aside from system architecture, we also need to evaluate the data. There are countless touchpoints that our systems are currently grasping, and it's up to us, or our systems, to draw the storylines across each dataset. Within that data lies immense information, each piece leading to a gold mine of new opportunities that our organization has yet to take advantage of.

Think of a digital transformation as an opportunity to get it right. It's an opportunity to scrub the data and make sure whatever is added to the new system is accurate and effective. To do that, we can either integrate our existing data or start clean.

This is an important decision to consider. Maybe there is a middle ground that would best accommodate historical trends integrated into the system. Whichever route we go, this decision will play a large role in the integration process.

The upside to migrating existing data to the new system is that it keeps the door open to consider historical data and trends. We will have the story of what has happened over the years, what trends have taken precedence, and what lessons we have learned from our past. We will have the story of our organization going back many years, which can help us see how we have progressed since we started.

The downside to migrating existing data is that we will have introduced a significant risk to the integration by bringing corrupt or dirty data over to a new and fresh system. If we do decide to migrate existing data, then we need to clean it and ensure its credibility before the migration.

On the other hand, we could start completely fresh. There are pros and cons to this approach as well. The upside is that this would dramatically simplify the implementation. We would also minimize the risk of dirty data, inaccurate or incompatible data, and other problems that could be created by migrating older data. What is not migrated will not be considered in the data moving forward. When looking for historical data, we would have to go back to old records to find the answers to a question that could have been answered more seamlessly if the work is done upfront during the digital transformation.

Through the process of evaluating how we want to migrate and manage our data, we will ideally develop a strong data plan. The reality is that it's very common for companies to have issues with data at go-live. Data migration is a multi-pronged task that needs attentiveness from every angle to make sure the transfer of data between systems is seamless. The transfer of data may sound simple on the surface, but understand that it includes, and is not limited to, all of the following elements:

- Data cleansing
- Data validation
- Data access protocols
- Data mapping
- Data exports
- Security

These elements must be thoughtfully considered and addressed. In our experience, many companies brush over these pieces. Many falsely deprioritize the deeper, subsurface elements of data migration when it's often one of the biggest obstacles to an ERP implementation.

Another important element to elaborate on, especially in today's landscape of cyber threats, is cybersecurity. Cybersecurity is an important output from our system architecture exercise. By outlining our system architecture in a similar diagram, as shown above, we will be able to identify how strong our cybersecurity efforts are around each system, but also between integration points. We won't dive too heavily into the world of cybersecurity here, but it is certainly something that should remain top of mind and should be accounted for in our implementation plan. We are living in an era of connectivity. Cyber threats are at an all-time high, and without intentional protection around our technology, processes, and people, the risk of a cyber attack is much greater.

Let's get back to system architecture. The diagram we rummage up will be a map that illustrates the future state system architecture. This system architecture diagram will ultimately help inform what our implementation strategy looks like. It will describe where customizations need to be made, if any, and any bolt-on functionalities that need to be tied in. It will outline the further needs of our implementation planning efforts to make sure we don't miss anything through the process. If we are replacing a specific piece of the puzzle, we will better understand what integration points and processes will be affected as a result of the new software implementation. We must figure out how to roll out the technology, what the sequences are, and what the priorities are. We also need a plan as we transition from phase one to phase two and beyond to fully understand what we are going to do with the interim systems that are temporarily in place.

Let me elaborate. Say we begin to break down our implementation plan into two phases. Phase one entails the replacement of our ERP software while keeping other systems in place. In phase two, we will replace the supply chain management system. Through that transition, we have to figure out what we

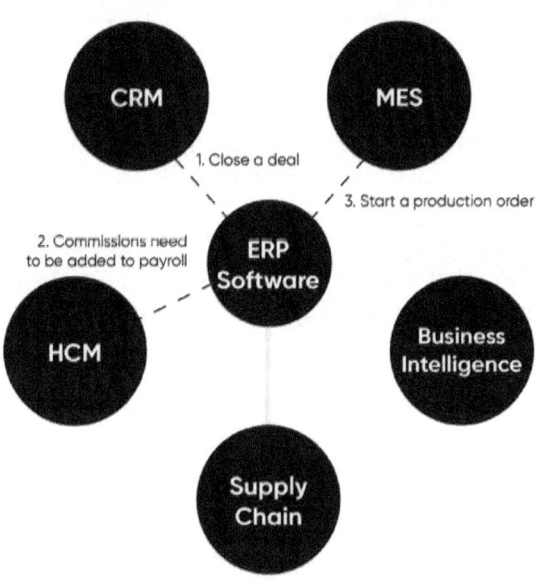

do with that touchpoint in the meantime. A good solution in this scenario would be to implement the new ERP software and build an *interim* integration point. Once we replace the supply chain management system, we will have to replace the interim integration point that was acting as a placeholder through the process. See the diagram below for this concept illustration.

This diagram will unveil countless plans and strategies on the technical side of our software implementation. Use it as a starting point to determine the tangible action plans that will get our current architecture to our future architecture.

Once we check off the ERP strategy, the OCM strategy, and the plan in which we will ensure our IT team is ready to handle what is coming, it's time to bring ourselves down to the reality of any digital transformation. There will always be inherent risks that come with high capital projects. No implementation plan is sound unless risk planning is incorporated into the greater formula. At the end of the day, we are the ones responsible for the outcome of our digital transformation, no one else. Not a consultant that helps us, not the system integrator, and certainly not the software vendor. We must take charge of our own fate by taking ownership of the ins and outs of the software implementation. Yes, it's okay to rely on our system integrator to configure and build technology to fit the need. However, nobody knows our company culture, our data, or our overarching business goals like the leaders within our own company. We should own it and govern the project, guiding it to the point that the outcome is what it was envisioned to be. Nobody else can do that for us.

Make a list of potential risks that come inherently to the transformation project. Maybe it's resource constraints, maybe it's a timeline, maybe it's the anticipated resistance that our team will experience. If we do not identify the potential risks ahead of time, they will sneak up and throw our project off balance. To piggyback off risk mitigation, it's also a powerful strategy to outline the framework of a few different implementation plans to compare the level of risks and pour into the one that best helps move the needle. Don't underestimate the correlation of a multi-strategy approach with ERP success.

When embarking on a digital transformation, there are a handful of implementation tactics we can choose from. These methodologies can often conflict with one another, making it difficult to know which methodology is right for our company. Whichever implementation plan we choose to follow, the goal is always to finish on time, on budget, and with the buy-in of our teams and executives. What might work well for one business may not work well for another, so as we evaluate the different implementation methodologies, we must evaluate them with the eye of our specific organizational characteristics. Various implementation methodologies act as the lens through which we look at our implementation plan. Each method carries its benefits and downfalls. Let's talk through the most common ones.

Agile

Agile is an approach that is focused on expediting the planning phase and instead jumping in with both feet. This methodology is based on testing and correcting. Even if it's just to a few people, this method encourages rolling out a new process or technology to see where it bends and breaks, and course correcting along the way. The goal with Agile is speed and agility. This approach enables the transformation team to acquire necessary feedback, build traction, and gain momentum as they implement new technology.

While this can be a great way to speed up a project and hit timelines, it can be counterintuitive to the goals organizations typically have as they walk into a technology implementation. Many organizations use their digital transformation to create a standard operating model or pivot to a new platform that will house new and old processes. Inherently, there is a conflict between the need to rapidly deploy technology and having common standard business processes and sound organizational change tactics.

Waterfall

This methodology is focused on outlining very defined, linear, and sequential phases of a project beginning with design and ending with go-live. With the waterfall approach, there is ample time spent planning and the project cannot move forward until each step is completed in the order it is planned to be completed. This often creates a sound architectural approach that enables project teams to cover all their bases. However, the risk of going over budget or beyond timelines is often most prevalent with this approach.

Lean Six Sigma

This approach is used across technology and operations. Lean Six Sigma is focused on clearly defined business processes, continuous improvement, measurement of business processes, decreasing waste, and increasing efficiency. This methodology focuses primarily on business process management and takes the opposite approach to Agile. This method also bases success primarily on metrics, and it values the continuous measurement and incremental improvement of operations along the way. The goal here is to become lean by finding the processes that will make operations the most effective. By optimizing processes and operational results for an organization, companies can drive growth in an efficient manner.

Change Management

This methodology comes to the forefront for organizations that value the human factor of a transformation. When considering methods like ADKAR, KODAR, or any other change management methodology, we easily notice the misalignment between the traditional methods, such as Agile. Change management methodologies focus on the *people* element of implementation rather than *processes* or *technology*. Instead of leveraging speed and efficiency, this method prioritizes impacts of the organization, proper organizational design, and tactics to deploy a change management strategy that ensures people come along for the ride. This approach is often an add-on to other methodologies on this list, and it's incorporated to create a cohesive implementation plan that covers all three pillars of digital strategy.

Customer Experience

This is another framework often used for digital transformation. A Customer Experience focused digital transformation is very much focused on the customer's journey from the moment they come in contact with our brand to the moment they receive our products or services rendered. What does it look like for the customer to interact with our organization? How can we optimize their experience? To do this correctly may require processes and procedures that aren't necessarily efficient in the name of maximizing the customer's experience.

For instance, take a company could automate customer service using an AI chatbox to field complaints and inquiries. This would save them time, money, and resources since the company wouldn't need as many Customer Service Representatives on the clock. For a company that is striving to deliver unmatched customer service, they will likely skip the AI-driven chat box and keep their Customer Service Representatives on the clock to provide a more personalized resolution to each customer's complaint or inquiry.

In this scenario, elements of our implementation that touch the front-facing facets of our processes and technologies may deviate from Lean Six Sigma. Instead, they may focus on ways to optimize consumer experience, regardless of any inefficiencies or delays that come with it. In this situation, it comes down to understanding the pieces of our business that are the most important to us. How do we differentiate? That will guide us as we determine the right methodology or mix of methodologies through our digital transformation.

Software Methodologies

A software integrator will come to the table with a recommended implementation plan. They often do not leverage Lean Six Sigma, nor do they bake in change management. Their approach will primarily be focused on acceleration and delivery. This can often result in costing more time and money down the line. As we set out toward implementation with a system integrator, it's critical to trust ourselves. We know the bare bones of our organizational needs, we are the ones with full working knowledge of our company culture, and we know what will work and what will not work. Rather than blindly accepting what system integrators tell us, we must understand the recommendations and add on or pivot to supplement their proposed methodologies to create a holistic implementation plan that fits our needs.

We could use certain pieces of each of these methodologies to formulate the perfect approach for our company. If we find conflict between different schools of thought, then we must deviate. There is no one right way or wrong way to implement new business practices and technologies. What matters is that it works for our business and that we are able to maintain and optimize our competitive edge through the change. They say failing to plan is planning to fail, and it couldn't be more true than when it comes to building out a strong implementation plan to help execute a digital strategy. These considerations should be addressed in the implementation plan and resolved well before we start our digital transformation journey. The more work we do upfront in planning these pieces, the more money and time we save through the transformation itself.

Chapter 23

Countdown to Launch

Once the implementation plan is solidified, it's time to start the design phase. By this point, we are crystal clear about the future state of our business processes and the general system architecture we have designed. We have laid the groundwork and are now preparing to launch into orbit.

Before we start the countdown, we want to make sure we address a handful of parallel considerations. One of those considerations is project governance, or making sure the project controls are in place to ensure that all these phases are being executed the way they should be. This should be outlined in our business case, and our business case will act as the guardrails once we set forth into the launch phase of our digital transformation.

There is also risk mitigation and risk management. This is meant to proactively identify risks before they become a problem so that the organization can mitigate and address them. Risk mitigation takes a lot of skill and is often deemed an art. More often than not, medium-sized and large organizations use outside consultants that specialize in ERP and enterprise software implementation to perform risk assessments from an objective point of view. There needs to be someone that can anticipate what the problems are before they become real problems that can't be fixed.

Finally, and arguably most importantly, is organizational change of management. The OCM strategy crafted earlier in the process runs the entire duration of the digital transformation project. Change management should start as early as the software evaluation and selection process and should continue post-go-live. Let's face it, at the end of the day, the human element is often the most difficult component of anything digital.

Once we can confidently say we have these elements locked in, it's time to start building and integrating the new technology into our system. This phase connects the dots between business needs and technical functionality and it brings our digital transformation to life. As we stand at the bridge that connects where we are today to where we are going, we must do our due diligence as we embark on the actual implementation and integration of the software we have selected. It all starts with the build.

Phase #1

Building

Now that the business processes have been defined and the software has been conceptually designed through our systems web, it's time to actually build it. This is where the technical resources come into play. The humility of bringing in an outside, third-party technical consultant is often what sets successful digital transformations apart from the rest. This third-party consultant will, ideally, start building the software to meet the specifications defined in the design phase.

Whether it's internal or a third party, this is the part of this process where the system will be integrated into the existing system architecture. The work will ultimately follow what has been designed in the web of the system that we discussed in the previous chapter. There may be different phases within this greater milestone depending on how much building, coding, and customizations need to be done.

Oftentimes, when system integrators are the only third-party assisting in the implementation, they will offer new and unique customizations, hoping to intrigue us with shiny-object syndrome. In many cases, it may seem like a great idea. Heck, the idea may even come from internal leadership. The reality is that any deviation from the original plan and scope of work will put the project at risk of going over timelines or over budget. No matter how great of an idea a bolt-on functionality or customization may seem, we must always defer to our project guardrails – the business case.

When we defer to the business case, we are going back to the goals and objectives we slated out before we even selected a software solution. The business case will tell us whether or not it's a good idea to chase something outside of the scope. Simply refer to the goals and objectives set forth in the business case. If the bolt-on functionality or customization will help us reach our future state goals faster or more efficiently and it won't completely butcher our budget, then we should do it. If it does not align with the values and expectations set forth in the business plan, then maybe it's something we revisit in the future.

At any rate, this is the most technical element of the entire digital transformation project, and far too often, it's the only element that organizations consider when implementing new software. Don't let that be you. This is one of the last pieces of the puzzle, and it always works best when the true due diligence has been mapped out and planned well in advance. When you take the approach of planning ahead, the "build" phase will be fairly quick and painless.

Phase #2

Testing

Once we have built the software and integrated it as we would like it to operate into our system architecture, it's time to test it and make sure it works properly. The goal here should be to break the system. We want to conceptualize and test the system in various ways to ensure it's ready before we go live. To begin, there are a few different components and iterations of the testing cycle. The first of that is called unit testing.

When undergoing **unit testing**, the focus is primarily on making sure that the technology itself works. Through this process, we will evaluate every microcosm and functionality of the overall technology. We want to make sure that no codes have been broken through customizations, confirm configurations across the entire system, and ensure that data is flowing through the system correctly. Unit testing ultimately comes down to testing different elements of the system itself to confirm functioning prior to moving on to the rest of the testing phases.

Once we can confirm that the system is, in fact, working correctly, then we move on to **integration testing**. This is where the individual pieces of the systems web are tested. We will explore how each integration of different systems works with the new software. This is typically done through end-to-end testing. Going back to the example of testing an order lifecycle from the moment the sale is closed to the manufacturing process entails multiple systems talking to one another. In this scenario, the CRM would likely transmit data to the ERP system, and the ERP system would distribute relevant information to the HCM system for commissions and payroll and to the WMS system for manufacturing.

In integration testing, we are testing end-to-end processes through the new system architecture. This exercise will highlight any areas that need attention and TLC before moving on to go live. The last thing we want to do is go live with a new system, only to have a broken integration somewhere within our system architecture, disrupting our operations as a whole. Once we have tested various scenarios, we can move on to user acceptance testing.

Business and **user acceptance testing**, often called conference room pilots, are less focused on technology and more focused on making sure that the business needs are being addressed. It also explores whether or not the business processes will work in a way that will tie in all three pillars of our transformation efforts: *People, processes,* and *technology*. Essentially, this element of testing will be a business simulation to determine what it would look like to use this technology within a production setting. This is the final phase of testing to make sure all looks good and the kinks are worked out before going live.

Testing is the single, most important element of preparing for go-live. As we go through each of the phases, follow these three rules of thumb.

1. *Test both functional and nonfunctional scenario requirements*

It's time to get creative and introduce scenarios that could cause problems. Again, our goal should be to break the system and find holes that might come up once our greater team is utilizing the new software. Make sure to also test the requirements, system architecture, and really every corner of the software as best we can.

2. *3x3 Rule*

Just like there are three pillars, we will want to test everything *3 times*. Depending on our technical specifics and requirements, we may need to test more than that. If our software is to be integrated with another software, those data flows need to be tested multiple times. Each time we make a change to the code, we need to test it multiple times. Yes, this sounds tedious, but this carries the ability to make or break the success of our digital transformation.

3. *Create test environments that mirror the actual scenarios the system will be utilized for*

By emulating software functions from an end-user perspective, we will be able to utilize real-life situational scenarios that the new system will have to accommodate. This is referred to as behavioral or black-box testing, and it touches on the user acceptance and functional aspects of the software. This will surface different types of issues – unlike white box testing that focuses on code structure, internal design, etc.

Phase #3

Go Live

Once various testing iterations are complete, it's time to go live. Believe it or not, a majority of ERP failures are due to go-live readiness, or lack thereof. It's time to turn on the new system and start using it in production. This is where we will revisit risk mitigation efforts. Before we go live, we should have a 'go/no go' checklist or checkpoint. It's simply a risk mitigation tool to make sure everything is ready to go live. After all, once we flip the switch, there is no going back. Having a checklist to make sure we have crossed all our T's and dotted all our I's will only help as we launch the new software for the world to see and use for themselves.

Two scenarios will play out here. Either the project is going to be successful and production is going to be seamless, or there is going to be some sort of disruption at the time of go-live. We're trying to avoid that, so it is important to have a checkpoint before going live to make sure the team has worked through, or at least considered, the risks associated with going live. Once that checkpoint has been reached, start the drum roll and flip the switch.

Phase #4

Post Go Live

The final step in the phase of implementation is post-go-live. A lot of organizations think they're done once they hit go live and they simply move on to the next thing. There are a few reasons why that is not the case. A lot of organizations crash and burn after launch as a result of the chaos that ensues due to some level of operational disruption. No matter what, there is going to be some degree of instability that happens at launch time. It could be very minimal and present itself as an opportunity for optimization, or it could be that our testing wasn't thorough enough and that our most in-demand product is on backorder for months.

No matter where we fall on that spectrum, post-go-live is often thought of as a stabilization phase. If there are operational elements that have been disrupted due to faulty integration points, then it will require all hands on deck, both internally and externally, to get things back on track. Simultaneously, we must address the people's side of the transformation.

People that don't understand the new system or have trouble in some capacity with the functionality of the system will need to be trained or retrained until things calm down. Until people are fully acclimated, then this constant touchpoint of training and communications needs to continue.

From there, it comes down to discovering optimization and business benefits. To reach the targeted ROI, we need to maximize the functionalities of the new software. Understandably so, when people get to go-live, they're so ready to be done with a project and they just want to move back to their day jobs. The problem is that looking at all the time and money spent leading up to this point, it would be foolish to just let it be. We must allocate some extra time to optimize business benefits and ensure a positive ROI.

When a satellite is launched from earth to space, all stakeholders are trained and prepared for anything. Anyone who has lived long enough knows that life just doesn't go according to plan sometimes. This applies to our software implementation as well. We can do our due diligence, cover all our bases, and still run into a hiccup at the time of rollout. That's why it's important to have a contingency plan in place that acts as our safety net at go-live.

Keep an ongoing plan of how to support the software beyond just going live. We'll need to know who to contact in case we need help, how we will contact them, and at what point to pull the plug and bring in a third party for help. Simply being prepared will not only bring ease of mind to the rollout, but it will help mitigate the 'deer in headlights' factor if something were to go wrong.

Chapter 24

Next Steps: Get Started on Software Implementation

Implementing new and emerging technology is no easy feat. With this era's robust and broad technology offerings, new software has the power to transform our business to operate at a higher level than ever before. On the other hand, it is easy to be overwhelmed by the complexity that certain software solutions can bring, and it can be even easier to fail to translate robust technology into a successful transformation.

Now that we've discussed all three pillars of digital transformation in detail, it's time to do it yourself. Take these steps to get started on your digital transformation, and refer to the preceding chapters as needed to refresh yourself on the best practices and tactics that come with each step.

Step 1

Develop a realistic view of time and cost.

Unrealistic expectations are some of the biggest mistakes you can make early on. If your expectations are misaligned internally, you will end up making poor decisions later on. For example, organizational change management is one of the first things to be eliminated from the scope of work, even though it is one of the most critical success factors you can invest in. You should avoid putting yourself in a position where you feel like cutting corners is a good idea, because it is never a good idea.

- The average software implementation costs three to five times the investment in software
- The average software implementation costs three to four percent of a company's annual revenue

These metrics might go up or down based on a number of complex factors. This initial implementation time and cost estimate should be refined based on the factors below.

Step 2

Define a phasing strategy that aligns with company culture.

Some companies intend for changes to happen quickly, but then they end up phasing the transformation in a way that dilutes that intent. Things like availability of internal resources, willingness to push team members to do whatever it takes to meet timelines (or not), and risk tolerance all factor into how appropriate an implementation strategy might be. An appropriate phasing strategy should ultimately align with your culture. This alignment is more important than any decision you can make.

Step 3

Understand the acceptable magnitude of process changes.

There's no doubt that the right technology will enable business transformations beyond your wildest expectations. However, that doesn't mean you should tackle too big of a change all at once. Instead, it might make more sense to

1. Define how much you're willing to change in actuality, not just what sounds good in theory.
2. Ensure that this project vision is consistent with the corporate strategy and vision.
3. Define an effective global change management strategy to manage the changes.
4. Adjust the phasing strategy and project scope as needed.

Once you have addressed this component, you can shift to executing, managing change, and ensuring overall alignment.

Step 4

Develop the internal and external resources plan.

Offering up sufficient internal resource support is one of the biggest challenges you will face in your software implementation. Most companies are fairly resource-constrained, so pulling the best talent out of daily operations is a real challenge.

The following steps will help you accomplish these things

1. Define clear roles and responsibilities between the organization and the system integrator.
2. Define the gaps between the resources needed and the resources that already exist.
3. Define the appropriate mix between internal and external roles (including onshore vs. offshore development resources).
4. Hire the internal and external resources that will support the project.
5. Adjust the project strategy and plan accordingly.
6. Hire resources to backfill the project team as needed.

If anything is going to slow down a digital transformation and cause budgetary overruns, lack of resources is one of the most likely. An effective resource plan will help mitigate this risk.

Step 5

Develop an Organizational Change Management plan.

The organizational changes required to enable a software implementation will be vast. The reality is that technology will be much easier to change than people or business processes. With this in mind, you will need to define an effective global organizational change management strategy to enable the overall transformation.

Your change strategy should include:

- Organizational readiness
- Communications
- Organizational design
- Training
- Executive and stakeholder alignment
- Benefits realization

- Workforce transition
- Cultural transformation

An effective organizational change and operational transition plan is the most important thing you can do to ensure project success.

Step 6

Define the IT transition strategy and plan.

You can't forget about your IT department. Even though this should be a business initiative rather than an IT-driven initiative, your IT department will be as impacted as anyone. They will require new skills, physical architectures, and training to effectively support the project in both the short and long term.

Here are some of the things that should be addressed as part of an IT transition plan:

- System architecture and integration points
- Application decommissioning plan
- Skills migration and training
- Reporting roles and responsibilities
- Project and post-go-live support processes (help desk support)
- Longer-term Center of Excellence plans

Remember that this is a group that will manage the environment long after the software consultants and project team members are gone. They must be prepared, and the time to prepare them is during the transformation project, not after.

Step 7

Build for software sustainability within the organization.

A digital transformation is a journey, not just a one-off project with a definitive start and end date. You need to plan and act accordingly. This should be addressed as part of your software project quality assurance work stream. Address this risk by developing and executing a software Center of Excellence strategy. Gartner describes effective CoEs as "concentrating existing expertise and resources in a discipline or capability to attain and sustain world-class performance and value."[5]

A center of excellence strategy will ensure that you have the appropriate factors in place:

- Software-specific knowledge transfer between your system integrator and internal project resources.
- A clear support plan beyond the digital transformation project itself.
- Better integration between your business operations and IT staff.
- A clear transition plan for your IT staff.
- A clear upgrade strategy and plan for the future.

If you're really in digital transformation for the long haul, then you'll need to build a sustainable organization to support that vision.

---

[5] "6 Steps to Building a Center of Excellence", Bizagi, June 10 2020, 6 Steps to Building a Center of Excellence (bizagi.com)

Chapter 25

Orbiting in the Third Stage

The Mars Exploration Rovers were sent to Mars in 2004. Their mission was to acquire data, photos, and other information that would help NASA decipher the conditions and history of the planet.[6] Whether it's a mission to Mars or a trip to the moon, there are a handful of systems and practices used to launch a rocket into space. A common practice is the three-stage-to-orbit launch system.

A rocket is usually built with three, distinct elements designed to facilitate the launch. This three-stage-to-orbit launch system is a common practice that enables rockets to go to the point of orbiting the Earth. The rocket uses three distinct stages to provide enough power and propulsion to get the giant, metal spacecraft into orbit. Each stage, or section, of the rocket, is stacked on top of the last, with the spacecraft sitting at the top. Come liftoff, each stage uses its fuel to get it to new heights. Once the first stage exhausts its fuel supply and is discarded, the second stage fires. This happens three times, and once the third stage commences, the spacecraft is in orbit (assuming it doesn't come crashing back down to Earth).

Similar to a rocket, there are three stages of digital transformation. To see success, we must do our due diligence and leverage the best practices and tactics discussed in this book. In the first stage, the project is just getting started. We have selected our software and implementation begins. In the second stage, the implementation is complete but is usually only at a fraction of the expected technical functionality, scope, and benefits. In the third stage, a cohesive digital and business transformation is complete. Full technical capabilities are realized, business processes are optimized, and the organization is aligned with the future state. Most importantly, business benefits and a positive return on investment are realized.

---

[6] "Mars Exploration Rovers Overview." NASA. NASA. Accessed August 30, 2022. https://mars.nasa.gov/mer/mission/overview/.

Much like a space rocket launch, the first two stages are important to get to the third, but optimal heights and speed aren't possible until the third stage launches the fastest and final rocket. The third stage booster can't be bogged down by inefficiencies and dead weight. If it is, it's at high risk of crashing back down to Earth. Clear best practices and expertise are required to overcome the gravitational pull of the current state.

A rocket takes time to design and build before it's ready for launch. The design and building phases are the prework to launch, just as they are in a digital transformation. The digital strategy we curate through the practices laid out in this book will act as our blueprint as we build our rocket for launch. Our digital transformation execution will follow this blueprint, and the level at which the blueprint is detailed will determine the level at which we see success.

We need all three stages, or pillars, to create a strong blueprint for our digital transformation. Our digital strategy needs to have equal parts of strategic intentions poured into our people, processes, and technology. We cannot remove or skimp on any one of the three pillars. The key is to invest just as heavily in the people side as we invest in the processes and technologies.

Everything within each pillar can be customized to fit our unique organizational needs, however, all three must amount to the same level of intention, effort, and relative investment. As each concept within this book is applied to our organization's digital transformation efforts, think of it in the framework of our organization's corporate or business strategy. Think of the entire process as a hierarchy that rolls into the corporate strategy. Once all three pillars support an overarching digital strategy that aligns and supports the corporate strategy, then you'll be in better shape than most.

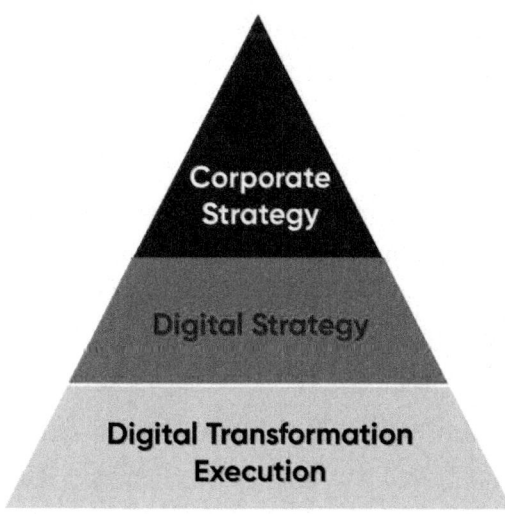

Now that we know what it takes to secure a strong digital transformation, let's look at a company that did it right. One of our clients at Third Stage Consulting Group came to us with a need for optimization. They were an international manufacturing company that was experiencing silos as a result of the various mergers and acquisitions it had evolved through. There was a disconnect among their international offices and they were experiencing bottlenecks in sharing information that inhibited collaboration across the organization.

They hired Third Stage Consulting to help them optimize their digital strategy and ultimately implement a new ERP system that would solve their problems. Our consultants performed a thorough organizational assessment to evaluate their processes, company culture, and current technological landscape. Through our assessment, we were able to garner a holistic understanding of their needs and help them create a digital strategy that would bridge the silos and drive efficiencies across their global enterprise.

In collaboration with their leadership team, we went beyond a simple software recommendation. We were able to fully dissect their prioritized processes to drive efficiencies and optimization toward their overarching strategic corporate goals. They designed and leveraged a strong organizational change management strategy to help their global team acclimate to the new processes and procedures with ease. Each element of the transformation started with an assessment: An operational assessment for their processes, an organizational assessment for their people, and a technical assessment for their technology. All assessments mirrored the steps and best practices we discussed together.

As a result of this due diligence, they realized that they didn't need half the systems that were being used. Rather, they were able to consolidate what once was multiple systems into one, overarching ERP system that integrated with the other systems already in use. The outcome was improved efficiencies, optimized communication and collaboration, and increased revenue.

This organization's leadership team was in full alignment from start to finish. They knew where they were going and why they were going there. They agreed on the requirements of the software as it related to their processes and people. As a result, they had a very positive digital transformation project.

As you begin your digital transformation journey, promise yourself that you will do your due diligence. Before jumping into a software implementation of any sort, take the time to marry your digital strategy to your corporate strategy. Take the time to process map and identify the gaps between your current and future state operating model. Take the time to grasp your company culture. Only then can you truly find the best fit technology that will launch your business to the moon.

The goal of any transformation initiative is to get the organization into a position where it can operate without friction. When your operations are at a high level and you can efficiently produce results, your efforts are then pointed toward improving your brand, service, and product quality. No longer are you subjected to bottlenecks and inefficiencies. You gain a competitive advantage. You improve your company culture. You grow your market share.

You orbit.

Acknowledgements

Diving deep into the expansive world of digital transformation has been an illuminating experience, one I couldn't have undertaken without the wisdom and support of countless individuals. I am deeply grateful to every brilliant mind and our supportive network that aided in bringing this work to life.

I extend heartfelt thanks to our Third Stage community and our consulting team. Their unwavering commitment to transparency and collective achievement stands as a testament to what we represent.

Also, thank you to my wife Kelly and my sons Cooper and Colton for supporting me on countless journeys throughout life and the digital transformation space over the years.

To you, the reader, a special thank you. The exploration of digital transformation is a shared voyage. As technology propels our world forward at an astounding rate, I hope this book acts as your guiding light, leading the way to a brighter, digital-centric future.

Stay connected and further our dialogue by following both my personal channels and Third Stage Consulting on social media. Tune into our weekly podcasts, Digital Stratosphere and Transformation Ground Control, which not only address trending topics in digital strategy but also provide a platform for listeners to ask questions. Find them wherever you enjoy your podcasts.

My team and I genuinely value direct interactions. If you're on a digital transformation journey and need a perspective or simply have feedback, do not hesitate to contact me at Eric.Kimberling@thirdstage-consulting.com. We also have countless free Digital Transformation and Organization Change Management playbooks on our website at thirdstage-consulting.com.

Cheers to our shared commitment to knowledge, understanding, and progress.

Eric

Citations

1. *"Top 10 Digital Transformation Failures of All Time, Selected by an ERP Expert Witness",* Third Stage Consulting Group, April 8, 2021, Top 10 Digital Transformation Failures of All Time, Selected by an ERP Expert Witness - Third Stage Consulting (thirdstage-consulting.com)
2. *"Estimated Number of Companies Worldwide from 2000 to 2021", Statista,* August 15, 2022, • Global companies 2021 | Statista
3. "What is SAP?", SAP.com website, accessed August 2022, https://www.sap.com/about/company/what-is-sap.html
4. "How Long Does It Take for an Architect to Draw Up Plans?" Denny + Gardner Remodeling Building Design Website, November 20, 2021, https://www.dennyandgardner.com/blog/how-long-architect-plans
5. "6 Steps to Building a Center of Excellence", Bizagi, June 10 2020, 6 Steps to Building a Center of Excellence (bizagi.com)
6. *"Mars Exploration Rovers Overview." NASA. NASA. Accessed August 30, 2022.* https://mars.nasa.gov/mer/mission/overview/.

Printed in Great Britain
by Amazon